Contents

D0307992

David Mamet: 1947–

1947 David Alan Mamet is born on 30 November in Chicago. His father, Bernard, is a labour lawyer, and his mother, Lenora, is a teacher.

1957 Mamet's parents separate and later divorce. Mamet lives with his mother and his younger sister, Lynn, in the South Shore area of Chicago and later in the Olympia Fields suburb. The pain of his parents' divorce is, in the view of some critics, reflected in much of his work, dealing with conflicts between men and women and difficulties in male/female relationships.

1963 –5 Mamet works as a waiter at Chicago's Second City and also backstage at the Hull House Theatre. Productions staged there include works by Harold Pinter, Brecht, and Edward Albee, all of whom will prove influential in his own work. He lives with his father in Chicago's Lincoln Park area, where he attends the Francis Parker Private School.

1965 –9 Mamet attends Goddard College in Plainfield, Vermont, where he earns a BA in English Literature. He studies acting with Sanford Meisner at the Neighborhood Theatre in New York. Jobs include working as a dancer with Maurice Chevalier's Montreal company, performing in *Toutes voiles dehours!!!* at the Autostade at Montreal's 1967 Expo, and working on a cargo boat on Lake Michigan. He completes early drafts of *Sexual Perversity in Chicago*, *Duck Variations*, and *Reunion*, and for his senior thesis, he writes *Camel*, a Second City-style revue.

1969 Mamet joins a theatre company at McGill University in Toronto, where he performs in Pinter's *The Homecoming*, serves as stage manager for the long-running off-Broadway hit, *The Fantasticks*, and works in a variety of other theatre jobs. He works as office manager in a Chicago real estate office.

1970 He accepts a position as acting instructor at Marlboro
      College, Vermont, where his play *Lakeboat* is first
      produced, directed by himself.

1971 He returns to Goddard College, as artist-in-residence and
      to teach acting. He forms the St Nicholas Theatre
      Company with two of his students. The company
      performs the first versions of *Duck Variations* and *Sexual
      Perversity in Chicago*, as well as a humorous piece based
      on Indian legends, *Lone Canoe*.

1972 The St Nicholas Theatre Company produces *Duck
      Variations* and *Sexual Perversity in Chicago* at a small
      theatre in Boston. Mamet returns to Chicago, where
      Duck Variations and the monologue *Litko* are performed
      as a double-bill at the Body Politic Theatre.

1973 Mamet plays a minor role in a production of *The Night
      They Shot Harry Lindsey With a 155mm Howitzer and
      Blamed it on Zebras*, produced by the Body Politic
      Theatre. He also works with a children's theatre
      company, which may have inspired some of his later
      writings for children.

1974 In June, *Sexual Perversity in Chicago* is presented by the
      Organic Theater Company at Chicago's Leo Lerner
      Theater, directed by Stuart Gordon. Mamet is artistic
      director of the St Nicholas Theatre Company, which
      presents *Squirrels* and *Mackinac* – a children's play – at
      the Bernard Horwich Jewish Community Center in the
      fall. *Sexual Perversity in Chicago* wins the Jefferson
      Award for Best New Chicago Play. Mamet serves as
      faculty member for the Illinois Arts Council. Gregory
      Mosher is appointed as assistant to the artistic director of
      the Goodman Theatre. He will become a close
      collaborator with Mamet over the years, directing many
      of his plays.

1975 *American Buffalo* premières at the Goodman Theatre's
      Stage Two, directed by Gregory Mosher and starring
      William H. Macy. In November, the St Nicholas
      Company produces Mamet's *Marranos*, a play about
      Jewish persecution during the Spanish Inquisition, at the
      Bernard Horwich Center. The theme of Jewish identity

will pervade much of Mamet's oeuvre, including his
fiction and non-fiction. *Sexual Perversity in Chicago*
opens at the off-off-Broadway St Clement's Theatre, in a
double bill with *Duck Variations*. *Sexual Perversity* wins
the Obie Award for Best New Play. St Nicholas moves
into a permanent theatre space on Halstead Street,
opening with *American Buffalo*. Mamet is visiting lecturer
at the University of Chicago, and contributing editor for
Oui magazine. He gives Meisner technique-based acting
classes, which will develop into a full training programme
for actors as well as designers, directors, and stage
managers. He writes *Revenge of the Space Pandas* for
New York's St Clement's Theatre.

1976 St Nicholas Theatre produces *Squirrels* and *Reunion*. In
January, *American Buffalo* opens at St Clement's Theatre,
winning an Obie Award as well as a Jefferson Award for
its Chicago run. Mamet resigns as artistic director of the
St Nicholas Company and moves to New York. *Sexual
Perversity in Chicago* and *Duck Variations* open at off-
Broadway's Cherry Lane Theatre. Mamet receives a New
York State Council of the Arts Grant, a Rockefeller
Award and a CBS Fellowship in Creative Writing, which
includes part-time teaching at Yale University.

1977 *American Buffalo* opens on Broadway in February,
winning the New York Drama Critics' Circle Award and
later enjoying another successful run at New York's
Théâtre de Lys. It marks an important development in
Mamet's career, with many critics recognising a vital and
unique new voice in the theatre. Goodman's Stage Two
Theatre presents *A Life in the Theatre*, with Joe
Mantegna, who will become another member of Mamet's
regular circle. Mamet directs *All Men Are Whores* at the
Yale Cabaret. In May, St Nicholas stages the première of
The Water Engine and later the première of *The Woods*,
which Mamet directs. Yale Repertory Theatre produces a
double bill of *Reunion* and *Dark Pony*. *The Revenge of
the Space Pandas or Binky Rudich* and *The Two-Speed
Clock* are produced by the Nicholas Children's Theatre as
well as in York, at Queen's Flushing Town Hall. *Duck*

Variations and *Sexual Perversity in Chicago* are produced at the Regent Theatre, London, the first European productions of Mamet's work, and run for six weeks. In December, Mamet marries actress Lindsay Crouse, who appears in many of his stage and film works.

1978 In January, *The Water Engine* is produced by Joseph Papp at the New York Shakespeare Festival Public Theater, transferring to Broadway, in a double bill at the Plymouth Theatre with *Mr Happiness*. Gregory Mosher, now artistic director of the Goodman Theatre, appoints Mamet as associate artistic director and writer-in-residence. *American Buffalo* is produced in June at London's National Theatre. *Prairie du Chien* is broadcast on BBC Radio as well as National Public Radio, which also hosts *The Water Engine*. Mamet wins the John Gassner Award for Distinguished Playwriting.

1979 Joseph Papp's Public Theater produces *The Blue Hour: City Sketches*, directed by Mamet, as well as *The Woods*. Chicago's Goodman Theatre premières *Lone Canoe, or the Explorer*, which is poorly received. More successful is a double bill of *Sexual Perversity in Chicago* and *A Sermon* at Chicago's newly opened Apollo Theater. *The Poet and the Rent* is produced at New York's Circle in the Square Repertory Theatre. PBS Television broadcasts *A Life in the Theatre*. *A Life in the Theatre* premières in London at the Open Space Theatre. In October, Mamet directs a triple bill at New York's Circle in the Square: *Reunion, Dark Pony*, and *The Sanctity of Marriage*. In December, New York's Ensemble Studio Theatre presents a short sketch, *Shoeshine*.

1980 Milwaukee Repertory Theater presents a revised version of *Lakeboat*. In New Haven, the Long Wharf Theatre stages a revival of *American Buffalo*, with Al Pacino. Mamet directs *Twelfth Night* at the Yale Repertory Theatre.

1981 Mamet's first screenplay is produced, an adaptation of James M. Cain's novel *The Postman Always Rings Twice*, directed by Bob Rafelson. He begins work on another film script, *The Verdict*. *Dark Pony* and *Reunion* are staged in London. *American Buffalo* transfers from the Long Wharf to Circle in the Square off-Broadway.

1982 *Lakeboat* is staged at New Haven's Long Wharf Theatre as well as Chicago's Goodman Theatre. *Edmond* premières at the Goodman Theatre and opens in New York, where it wins the Obie Award. *The Verdict* is released in December, and Mamet is nominated for an Academy Award for Best Adapted Screenplay.

1983 In September, the world première of *Glengarry Glen Ross* takes place at the National Theatre in London, winning the prestigious Society of West End Theatres Award (SWET) for Best New Play, as well as the Olivier Award. The Goodman Theatre stages Mamet's adaptation of *Red River* by Pierre Laville. Goodman Studio produces a triple bill, including Mamet's *The Disappearance of the Jews*. The New York Ensemble Theatre's Marathon Festival of One-Act Plays presents five of Mamet's sketches as *Five Unrelated Pieces*. *Three by Three*, another collection of sketches, is presented in July at New York's Park Royal Hotel and includes Mamet's *The Dog*. *American Buffalo*, with Al Pacino and J. J. Johnston, moves to Broadway. Mamet publishes a children's play, *The Frog Prince*.

1984 In February, the Goodman Theatre stages the American première of *Glengarry Glen Ross*. In March it transfers to Broadway, running for 378 performances and winning the Pulitzer Prize, the Drama Critics' Award for Best American Play, a Joseph Dintenfass Award, and four Tony nominations, including Best Play and Best Director for Gregory Mosher. *American Buffalo* opens at the Duke of York's Theatre, London. *The Frog Prince* opens at Milwaukee Repertory Theater, and the Ensemble Studio Theatre features *Vermont Sketches* as part of its second Marathon Festival of One-Act Plays. Mosher and Mamet create the New Theatre Company (NTC), an independent company featuring many of Mamet's regular associates.

1985 The New Theatre Company premières its season with Mamet's adaptation of *The Cherry Orchard* at the Goodman Studio. NTC later moves to a new venue, the Briar Street Theatre, where it produces *The Shawl* and a one-act play, *The Spanish Prisoner*, which will evolve into a major motion picture. In March, Chicago radio station WNU of Northwestern University broadcasts *Goldberg Street* and *Cross Patch*, featuring NTC members. British television's *South Bank Show* produces a programme on Mamet. Gregory Mosher is named artistic director of New York's Lincoln Center, and his first production is a double bill of *Prairie du Chien* and *The Shawl*. The film *About Last Night*, loosely based on *Sexual Perversity in Chicago*, is released. *Edmond* receives its European première at the Newcastle Playhouse, co-produced by the Royal Court Theatre, to which it transfers in December. Mamet writes *Vint* for the American Repertory Company's touring production of *Orchards*, a collection of sketches by contemporary playwrights based on Chekhov's short stories. Mamet and Macy found the Atlantic Theater Company in New York. Mamet publishes *A Collection of Dramatic Sketches and Monologues*.

1986 Mamet wins Academy Institute Award in Literature. *Prairie du Chien* and *The Shawl* are staged at the Royal Court Theatre Upstairs. *Writing in Restaurants*, a collection of Mamet's essays, is published.

1987 Mamet writes screenplay for *The Untouchables*. Also writes and directs *House of Games* – his first film as writer and director – which wins a Golden Globe Nomination for Best Screenplay. Mamet writes an episode for the TV show *Hill Street Blues*.

1988 American Repertory Theatre stages Mamet's adaptation of *Uncle Vanya*, featuring the NTC members. *Speed-the-Plow* opens at the Royale Theatre on Broadway. With Shel Silverstein, Mamet undertakes his second film as writer-director, *Things Change*, which opens the London Film Festival. Mamet's sketch *Where Were You When It Went Down?* is part of an off-Broadway revue, *Urban Blight*, directed by John Tillinger. Mamet directs *Sketches of War* at Boston's Colonial Theatre, a programme that includes Mamet's *Cross Patch*. For *The Untouchables*, Mamet earns a Writers Guild Award Nomination for Best Screenplay Based on Material from Another Medium. His children's book, *Warm and Cold*, is published.

1989   In January, *Speed-the-Plow* opens at London's National Theatre. That summer, a work-in-progress, *Bobby Gould in Hell*, receives a staged reading at the National Theatre; in December, the completed play premières at Lincoln Center's Mitzie Newhouse Theater. *The Water Engine* receives its British première at London's Hampstead Theatre Club. In October, the West End's Theatre Royal, Haymarket, stages a major revival of *A Life in the Theatre*, following a United Kingdom tour. Mamet writes another screenplay, this one for Neil Jordan's film remake, *We're No Angels*. Mamet's second collection of essays, *Some Freaks*, is published.

1990   Atlantic Theater Company performs Mamet's adaptation of Chekhov's *Three Sisters* at Philadelphia's Festival Theater. Another Mamet adaptation of Chekhov, *Uncle Vanya*, premières at the Harrogate Theatre in Britain as well as at the Goodman Theatre in the US. Mamet completes screenplays for *Hoffa, the Deer Slayer* (based on a James Fenimore Cooper story), *High and Low* (based on a film by Akira Kurosawa), and *Ace in the Hole*. Mamet appears on the BBC TV's *Clive James Show*. His collection of poetry, *The Hero Pony*, is published.

1991   Mamet writes and directs the film *Homicide*. His book, *On Directing Film*, is published.

1992   *Oleanna* premières at New York's American Repertory Theatre, moving to the Orpheum Theatre. Writes screenplay for *Glengarry Glen Ross*. Publishes a book of essays, *The Cabin: Reminiscence and Diversions*.

1993   British première of *Squirrels* staged at King's Head Theatre, Islington. TNT American television films *A Life in the Theatre*, with Matthew Broderick and Jack Lemmon. *Oleanna*, directed by Harold Pinter, is staged at London's Royal Court Theatre, transferring later to the Duke of York's in London's West End.

1994   Mamet writes and directs the film version of *Oleanna*, starring William H. Macy and Debra Eisenstadt. *The Cryptogram*, directed by Gregory Mosher, premières at London's Ambassadors Theatre. Sam Mendes directs a

revival of *Glengarry Glen Ross* at London's Donmar
Warehouse. *Vanya on 42nd Street*, Mamet's adaptation of
Chekhov's work, opens in New York, directed by André
Gregory. Mamet publishes three books: his novel *The
Village, A Whore's Profession: Notes and Essays*, and *A
Life With No Joy In It, and Other Plays and Pieces*.

1995   *The Cryptogram*, directed by Mamet, premières at
Boston's C. Walsh Theatre as well as in New York at the
Westside Theatre Upstairs. Mamet's piece *An Interview* is
included in a three-act show, *Death Defying Acts*, staged
at the Variety Arts Theatre in New York. Mamet directs
his adaptation of J.B. Priestley's *Dangerous Corner* at
New York's Atlantic Theater Company.

1996   Film version of *American Buffalo*, with screenplay by
Mamet, opens the Boston Film Festival. To celebrate its
twenty-fifth anniversary and long collaboration with
Mamet, the Ensemble Studio Theatre stages five one-acts
and monologues, including *No One Will Be Immune* and
the New York première of *Joseph Dintenfass*. Mamet
publishes another book of essays, *Make-Believe Town:
Essays and Remembrances*.

1997   *The Old Neighborhood* premières at the American
Repertory Theatre in Cambridge, Massachusetts, then
moves to Broadway at the Booth Theatre. The film *Wag
the Dog* opens, with a screenplay by Mamet and Hilary
Henkin, and is nominated for a Golden Globe Award for
Best Motion Picture, Best Screenplay, and Best Actor. It
also receives an Academy Award nomination for Best
Adapted Screenplay as well as a nomination for Best
Screenplay by the Writers Guild of America. Mamet
writes and directs *The Spanish Prisoner*, which opens the
Toronto Film Festival. Writes an original screenplay, *The
Bookworm*, which is produced as the film *The Edge*.
Publishes a book on acting, *True and False: Heresy and
Common Sense for the Actor*; *Three Uses of the Knife:
On the Nature and Purpose of Drama*, essays originally
delivered as the Columbia Lectures on American Culture;
also a historical novel, *The Old Religion*.

1998   Two Mamet plays receive their British premières:

Lakeboat at London's Lyric Studio, Hammersmith, and *The Old Neighborhood* at the Royal Court at St Martin's Lane. *Jade Mountain* opens at the New York Ensemble Theatre's Marathon of One-Acts. Mamet's screenplay for *Ronin* is directed by John Frankenheimer. Mamet directs his film adaptation of Terence Rattigan's play, *The Winslow Boy*. He co-produces his screenplay *Lansky*, which is broadcast on HBO Television.

1999 Mamet directs the première of his *Boston Marriage* at the American Repertory Theatre. Writes screenplay for *The Cincinnati Kid*. Publishes *Jafsie and John Henry: Essays on Hollywood; Bad Boys and Six Hours of Perfect Poker*; a work of fiction, *Bar Mitzvah* and *The Chinaman*.

2000 The Donmar Warehouse, London, stages a revival of *American Buffalo* by the Atlantic Theater Company. In September, Mamet's film of Samuel Beckett's *Catastrophe* premières at the Toronto International Film Festival, featuring Harold Pinter as well as John Gielgud in his final film performance. *State and Main*, a film written and directed by Mamet, opens in December; among the honours it receives are the National Board of Review 2000 Best Ensemble Performance award as well as a nomination for Best Screenplay.

2001 The British première of *Boston Marriage* is staged at the Donmar Warehouse, London, directed by Phyllida Lloyd. *State and Main* is nominated for the Chicago Film Critics Award. *Heist*, the eighth film written and directed by Mamet, premières at the Venice Film Festival in August. *Speed-the-Plow* is staged at the Edinburgh Festival. A film version of *Lakeboat*, directed by Joe Mantegna, is released for limited general distribution. Mamet's futuristic novel, *Wilson: A Consideration of the Sources*, is published. The film *Hannibal*, with screenplay by Mamet and Steven Zaillian and directed by Ridley Scott, is released.

2002 Mamet publishes *South of the Northeast Kingdom*, a collection of essays.

Plot

The play is divided into two acts, the first containing three scenes – all of which take place in different booths at a Chinese restaurant – and the second act consisting of one scene only, set in the now ransacked real estate office.

At the opening of the play, John Williamson, manager of the real estate office, and Shelly Levene, a salesman past his prime, are in heated discussion about Levene's need to obtain good 'leads'. Levene is desperately trying to convince Williamson – who is about ten years his junior – of his effectiveness as a salesman by pointing to his past successes, despite his recent downturn in luck. Frantic to obtain the premium 'leads' that will give him the edge in an aggresive sales contest, Levene pumps up his own accomplishments and points out that he was with the firm long before Williamson, but he is ultimately reduced to begging his boss and finally bribing him for the information, although Levene doesn't have the cash to complete the deal. This opening scene reveals the pathos of Levene's situation along with Williamson's indifference, and, more importantly, establishes the cut-throat nature of the real estate world into which the play delves.

The scene shifts to a discussion between two other salesmen, Dave Moss and George Aaronow, both in their fifties, who have just finished dinner. They are discussing the real estate contest, in which the first prize is a Cadillac, the second prize a set of steak knives, and the last two men will be fired. Lamenting the frustrations of getting worthwhile leads, Moss curses the uselessness of trying to sell to certain ethnic groups, airing his unbridled prejudices against 'Polacks and deadbeats' and anyone from India. The verbal exchange, a brilliant illustration of Mamet's cryptic dialogue, indicates Moss's superiority over Aaronow, with Moss dominating the conversation and Aaronow doing little more than echo his colleague's language. The scene also illustrates Mamet's chilling use of language as a tool of manipulation: Moss, arguing the immorality of how employees are treated, insidiously weaves a scheme to rob the central office, implicating Aaronow in the plan. When Aaronow asks how he has come to be an accomplice in this potential crime, Moss responds, 'Because you listened.'

The closing scene of Act One comprises yet another conversation, this one between strangers: ace salesman Ricky Roma and a lone drinker, James Lingk, whom Roma eyes as a potential customer – or more precisely, victim. Again, the scene demonstrates the manipulative power of language as Roma gradually establishes a kinship with Lingk to engage his confidence. In a long monologue that is a *tour de force* of deceptive confidentiality, Roma ruminates on the meaning of life and what it all amounts to. Act One ends as Roma 'shares' with Lingk his information about Glengarry Highlands in Florida; his final words are, 'Listen to what I'm going to tell you now:'. The word 'listen' echoes the chilling conclusion of Scene Two, when Aaronow finds himself helplessly implicated in a robbery scheme because he 'listened'.

All of Act Two takes place the next day in the real estate office, which has been ransacked. 'A broken plate glass window boarded up, glass all over the floor'. Throughout the act, a detective is interviewing the various salesmen to find out who committed the robbery. Roma enters in great distress over whether the contract he had persuaded Lingk to sign had been stolen with the others. When Williamson assures him that the contract is safe, Roma exults, 'Then I'm over the fucking top and you owe me a Cadillac. [. . .] And I don't want any fucking shit . . .'. Aaronow worries over whether the contracts were insured as well as his own failure as a salesman, but Roma encourages him, saying he just 'had a bad month'. However Roma is also upset that he must now go out and reclose all his other contracts and angrily rejects Williamson's offer to give him the previous year's leads, especially since they include one named Patel, an Indian. Roma is further aggravated that he has to waste time talking to the police, who, in his view, are '*stupid*'.

Meanwhile, Levene charges in exultantly, announcing that

he's sold $82,000 worth of land, putting him 'over the top' for the Cadillac. When Moss merely mocks Levene, Roma attacks Moss for having no sales himself, noting that when Moss does make a sale, he brags insufferably. As this heated exchange continues, Levene attempts to recreate the kitchen scene at the home of the Nyborgs, the couple with whom he closed his deal. When Moss storms out, Roma patiently listens to Levene's celebratory, nostalgic tale. 'Like in the *old* days, Ricky. [. . .] Like, like, like I *used* to do . . . I did it.' Levene's new-found confidence prompts him to strike out at Williamson, reminding him that in the old days he wasn't even around and cautioning that he may lose his job. He also demands three good leads from Williamson.

Suddenly, Roma spots James Lingk outside the door and quickly fabricates a scenario, telling Levene to pose as a client to whom he has just sold five waterfront plots at Glengarry Farms. As Lingk enters, Roma is speaking of the property's value; Lingk interrupts to say 'I've got to talk to you.' Roma welcomes him, telling Levene that he has 'just put Jim into Black Creek' in Florida, to which Levene responds impressively. As Lingk continually tries to get Roma's attention, Roma raves about the value of Jim's land and says that Levene – whom he introduces as Mr Morton – is the European Sales and Services Director for American Express. Lingk tells Roma his wife has demanded that he get his cheque back, Roma attempts to end the conversation on the pretext that he must take 'Mr Morton' to the airport and that he will meet with Lingk the following week. Concerned that the three-day grace period, during which the contract can be cancelled, will have expired, Lingk says that he must talk to Roma now or that he will have to contact the State Consumer's Attorney. Roma assures him that his cheque has not been cashed and that his 'grace period' will still be in place the following week, since weekends do not count as part of the three days.

Meanwhile, mayhem continues with the police interrogations. Aaronow emerges from the office distraught over how he has been treated. 'No one should talk to a man that way,' he says. 'I *work* here, I don't come in here to be *mistreated*. [. . .] I meet *Gestapo* tactics.' Williamson, in frustration, demands that

Aaronow get out, go to lunch, and stop disrupting the office. The detective, Baylen, then summons Levene, who is trying to make an exit in order to preserve his cover for Roma, and then calls for Roma, who is desperately trying to keep Lingk from leaving while fending off the authorities. Again, he appeals to Lingk, telling him to '*forget* the deal' and to confide in him his real concerns. But Lingk gradually becomes aware that something has happened; Williamson refers to the incident as merely 'a slight burglary' and assures Lingk that his contract is safe and that his cheque has been cashed. At that point, the desperate Lingk heads for the door, telling Roma not to follow him. Infuriated, Roma curses Williamson for ruining his six-thousand-dollar deal in what is perhaps the most powerful diatribe in the play. 'I'm going to have your *job*, shithead. [. . .] What you're hired for is to *help* us – does that seem clear to you? To *help* us. *Not* to fuck us up.'

   During Roma's invective, Levene emerges from his inter-rogation and reiterates Roma's feelings towards Williamson, who is confidently unmoved, muttering only, 'Mmm'. But in his own raging, Levene makes a serious error – again through language – that is to seal his fate. When he says to Williamson, 'You're going to make something up, be sure it will *help* or keep your mouth closed', Williamson calls him on the point, noting that in truth, he had *not* taken the contracts to the bank the previous evening. 'One night a year that I left a contract on my desk. Nobody knew that but *you*. Now how did you know that?' He accuses Levene of having committed the robbery and demands to know what he did with the leads. Levene denies the accusation but slowly crumbles; when Williamson promises immunity in return for the information about the leads, Levene caves in and admits he sold them to their real estate competitor Jerry Graff and that Moss was in on the deal with him. Not surprisingly, Williamson reneges on his promise and prepares to inform the police about Levene's confession. Levene desperately tries to bribe Williamson, as he had at the beginning of the play, but Williamson rejects the offer. Levene offers him a cut of all his sales, including the $82,000 deal he had sealed that morning, but Williamson cruelly disabuses him of the notion that the sale had any value, noting that the Nyborgs are notoriously insane and that their cheque is worthless. 'They just like talking to salesmen,' he says. When Levene asks Williamson why he is throwing him to the wolves, Williamson replies coldly, 'Because I don't like you.' Roma emerges from the office and, knowing nothing about Levene's part in the robbery, says he admires Levene's use of the old sales techniques, why don't they go into partnership? Baylen summons Levene and it transpires that Roma intends to cut in on Levene's future profits. As the play ends, Aaronow returns and says, 'Oh, god I hate this job', while Roma exits to go to the Chinese restaurant where the play began.

Commentary

Mamet and the American theatre

Before the age of thirty, David Mamet had already established himself as a major new presence in the American theatre and has since become one of its foremost, influential and provocative playwrights. A writer very much in touch with the pulse of American life, he is noted for his unique and distinctive voice, and indeed, it is difficult to miss the mark of his gritty street language, his exploration of the grimy underworld corners of American society, the cadence of his powerful and pulsing language, and the familiar trickster characters who people his plays. Along with such playwrights as Sam Shepard, Edward Albee, Arthur Miller, Tennessee Williams, and Eugene O'Neill, Mamet explores the mythology that has shaped America, mythology ranging from the ideal family, to rugged individualism, to the dream of material success as the road to happiness. But Mamet – a native of Chicago – is also a distinctly urban writer, and his plays are often charged with the energy, brutality, and sense of dislocation wrought by city life.

Mamet brings to the theatre a world dominated primarily by men, in settings that are traditionally male-oriented, such as pool halls, porn theatres, smoky poker dens and cheap bars, with characters who curse, cheat, gamble, and scheme. For the most part, women have been absent or peripheral in his plays, although later works such as *The Cryptogram* and *Boston Marriage* (a Victorian-style comedy with no male characters) place them more at the forefront. Because of this tendency Mamet has sometimes been charged with being gender-biased and even misogynistic but such views seem unjust, given that he is writing about a world with which he is familiar. In *A Whore's Profession*, Mamet points out that he doesn't '*know* anything about women' and that when he realised '*they* were people too', he then spent years trying to figure out what their 'thoughts and feelings *are*'. Besides, most of the men he depicts are not particularly likeable, being gangsters, con artists, thieves or pathetic losers. Furthermore, women who do appear often wield power, such as Joan and Deborah in *Sexual Perversity in Chicago*, who expose the shallowness of Danny and Bernie, Carol in *Oleanna*, who destroys her professor's life, and Karen in *Speed-the-Plow*, who very nearly disrupts a business deal between two Hollywood moguls. More significantly, these dismal gender situations point to a recurring theme in Mamet's plays, that of the troubled relationships between men and women.

Perhaps Mamet's central contribution to American theatre is the language of his plays, which often underscores his gritty male milieu. His characters typically speak in crude gutter talk, as in this exchange between Teach and Don in *American Buffalo*:

> **Teach**   Guys like that, I like to fuck their wives.
> **Don**   I don't blame you.
> **Teach**   Fucking *jerk* . . .
> **Don**   (I swear to God . . .) (Methuen, 2002, p. 27)

While such language seems starkly realistic – and indeed is to a great extent – it is also highly poetic. As Mamet has pointed out, people don't talk in real life as they do in his plays, though he makes the dialogue sound like they do. But he carefully sculpts the words into a rhythmic, sometimes musical style that is a distinctive mark of his work, not only the harsh, crude pieces but also gentler plays such as *Dark Pony*, *Boston Marriage* and *A Life in the Theatre*. Furthermore, Mamet's language shapes and defines his plays and his characters. In *Edmond*, for instance, the fragmented nature of the language as well as the play's twenty-three incongruous scenes reflects the disjointed quest of the main character for some kind of meaning in his life and the abrupt, disconnected experiences he undergoes. In *Glengarry Glen Ross*, the language drives the characters, defines them, and provides them the means for both existence and even survival.

Mamet's language also furthers the influence of Absurdist drama in American theatre. He has acknowledged Samuel

Beckett and Harold Pinter as two major influences on his work, and the sparseness, abruptness, and absences of his stage language, as well as a sudden eruption of violence, a sense of some unknown menace, the disparity between appearance and reality and the failure of communication, clearly indicate the mark of his predecessors. But in their structure and thematic content, Mamet's plays are not so close to the Absurdist writers, whose plays reflect in form the essential meaninglessness of existence. Mamet, by contrast, is a strong proponent and practitioner of the well-made play, against which Theatre of the Absurd rebelled, and his plays are classically and conventionally structured. Furthermore, rather than sharing their existentialist concerns, Mamet focuses on the loss of spirituality and community in American life as well as the degrading effects of American business and materialism. His work laments a world where greed and egotism rule and where the attempt at human connection too often fails. Although his plays don't subscribe to the essential philosophy of Absurdist drama – that life is purposeless and random – they do cull certain elements of American life to expose their artificiality and pointlessness. In *Glengarry Glen Ross*, for example, the element of salesmanship represents the need for survival, a need for which some of the characters are struggling to find reasons, however frail. In *Edmond*, the central character is searching for a way to fit into a world that seems to have no place for him, and in *Oleanna*, Carol's initial attempt to understand her professor's class material through conversations with him ultimately turns into a deadly menace through the manipulation of language.

The element of role-playing in American theatre takes a distinct form in Mamet's work, primarily through the figure of the con artist. Although other playwrights also treat this theme in particular ways – Tennessee Williams, for instance, depicts characters living in the haze of illusion, while Edward Albee often shows them trapped within their social status – Mamet develops it through the trickster who is sometimes humorous but always an exploiter of unsuspecting victims. This concept is clearly evident in *Glengarry Glen Ross*, in which the goal of the salesmen is to sell worthless land to unsuspecting

customers, using whatever unscrupulous methods they can
conjure. Ricky Roma is the astute master of this game, as
evidenced by his smooth manipulation of James Lingk through
the guise of friendship. *American Buffalo* revolves around a
pathetically comic failure to swindle a coin collector out of his
presumably valuable set, but it also traces Teach's attempt to
con his way into the deal while pushing Bob out. Perhaps the
most explicit illustration of the con artist is Mamet's film
House of Games, in which a master con artist teaches the art
to a woman novice, only to have her ultimately turn the tables
and con him in a deadly conclusion.

On the other hand, many of Mamet's characters, while
playing roles, are storytellers without any subversive agenda,
except perhaps to deceive themselves, to shape or reshape their
own lives and past into a comforting fiction that serves as a
buffer against isolation, or at least to connect to a past that
seems to have disappeared from the national consciousness. In
the touching short play *Dark Pony*, a father recounts a
mythical tale of an Indian brave to his young daughter as they
drive home in the dark, a story he's obviously comforted her
with many times. Similarly, *Lone Canoe, or the Explorer* also
addresses the mythical view of native Americans. The
storytelling impulse is more desperate and narcissistic in plays
such as *Sexual Perversity in Chicago*, in which Danny and
Bernie need to detail the episodes in their mundane lives as a
way of infusing them with some sense of importance, however
self-delusional, ostensibly playing roles to impress others but
deceiving only themselves. The two actors in *A Life in the
Theatre*, Robert and John, literally play roles in their onstage
scenes, illustrating Mamet's concept that theatre is very much
about storytelling, but even offstage they relate to one another
through their respective roles of 'an older actor' and 'a younger
actor'. Even in *Glengarry Glen Ross*, Levene feels the need to
recount in great narrative detail his closing a contract with the
Nyborgs, which he believes has been a financial windfall but
which of course turns out to be worthless. Again, his
storytelling acts as a means for him to verify his own sense of
importance and even justify his existence.

Because of Mamet's emphasis on language over plot, some

critics have found his plays deficient in their lack of action (a characteristic that also links Mamet to Theatre of the Absurd). But his plays emphasise internal rather than external development, and tension develops through the shifting relationships within and among the characters. As discussed in 'Mamet's language and style', language for Mamet *is* action and emotion; characters exist and define themselves through what they say or fail to say, by their inarticulacy or long, explosive speeches. It is, in fact, Mamet's particular blend of language and territory with his views of skewed American values and spiritual desolation that give his plays such a distinct and remarkable originality.

Mamet's career

Mamet came to playwriting in a rather haphazard way and notes that he had never set out consciously to pursue the craft. As a teenager in his native Chicago he had worked as a busboy at Second City, a prominent comedy club that has spawned many renowned performers, including Bill Murray, Gilda Radner, Dan Aykroyd, and Alan Arkin (who starred in the film version of *Glengarry Glen Ross*). Although Mamet himself never performed with the club's improvisational troupe, his experience there would provide material for his first play, *Camel*. During his undergraduate career at Goddard College, Vermont, where he was majoring in English and spending a lot of time with theatre groups, Mamet took time off to study acting under Sanford Meisner at New York's Neighborhood Playhouse School of the Theatre. Although an acting career never panned out, he was deeply influenced by the Stanislavski acting method he learned and by the Russian director's concept of language, which was to inform most of Mamet's subsequent work in both stage and film. Mamet has remarked on his fascination – derived from Meisner and Stanislavski – with the correlation between language and behaviour, noting how language determines human behaviour rather than the other way around – that what we say determines how we act. In *Glengarry Glen Ross*, for example, the behaviour of salesman Ricky Roma in his engagement with Lingk is driven and shaped by his silver-tongued language of persuasion. Later, however, when Williamson unwittingly spoils the deal, Roma lashes out at his boss like a cobra, with a now brutal language that again generates his manner.

During his New York sabbatical, Mamet also worked as a lighting operator and stage manager with the long-running off-Broadway hit, *The Fantasticks*, an experience he considers valuable. During his time at Goddard, Mamet began writing plays, turning out early drafts of *Sexual Perversity in Chicago*, *Duck Variations*, and *Reunion*. When the time came to write his senior thesis, Mamet asked if he could write a play instead, a request to which his adviser – much to Mamet's surprise – readily agreed. The result was a revue, *Camel*.

Upon graduation, Mamet returned to Chicago, where he drove a cab and did other odd jobs. Through connections with friends, he landed a temporary teaching position back in Vermont, at Marlboro College, listing as one of his credentials a play he hadn't even written, *Lakeboat*, but which he completed by the time he arrived, subsequently staging a successful production at Marlboro. Comprising twenty-eight scenes, *Lakeboat* takes place on a Merchant Marine ship sailing the Great Lakes, territory familiar to Mamet. Along with its Chicago milieu, the play portends many aspects of his later work, including a cast that is all male and characters whose lives are empty and desolate beneath their boasting and crude talk.

After his stint at Marlboro, Mamet returned to his native Chicago, where he worked in a real estate office, an experience that was to provide the grist for his Pulitzer Prize-winning play *Glengarry Glen Ross*. In his 'Author's Note' to the published edition, Mamet describes the office as 'a fly-by-night operation which sold tracts of undeveloped land in Arizona and Florida to gullible Chicagoans', urging them to 'Get in on the ground floor' of this fabulous opportunity. His job, he goes on to explain, was to call back prospective customers, 'assess their income and sales susceptibility, and arrange an appointment with them for one of the office salesmen'. Meanwhile, Mamet continued to work on another play, which he proposed to Goddard College for possible production. He was subsequently invited to teach an acting class there and ended up spending two years as artist-in-residence, during which time he wrote and produced several plays. Mamet considers this period crucial because of the time it allowed him to work and experiment in honing his craft; in fact, he has said that this 'was probably the most precipitous point in my career as a playwright, because it gave me a laboratory to constantly produce. It was invaluable.' Another important event during his time at Goddard was his formation of a small acting group, the St Nicholas Theatre Company, which produced his plays as well as those of such established playwrights as Eugene O'Neill.

Returning to Chicago, Mamet settled into a period which was to shape him as a major playwright and to define him as essentially a Chicago writer. Mamet, in turn, was to help establish Chicago itself as a serious theatrical city. *Sexual Perversity in Chicago*, for example, is set in 'Various spots around the north side of Chicago, a big city on a lake'. Several of his own plays were performed by various companies, including the Body Politic, an experimental troupe, and the Bernard Horwich Jewish Community Center Youth Theatre. Mamet also re-formed the St Nicholas Company as the St Nicholas Players, serving as its artistic director. The culmination of this intensive period came in 1974, when *Sexual Perversity in Chicago*, performed by Organic Theatre, won an award as best new Chicago play of the year. When it moved to New York the following year, produced as a double bill with *Duck Variations* at the off-off-Broadway St Clements Theatre, it won the Obie Award for best new play of the year. Subsequently it moved to the off-Broadway Cherry Lane Theatre, and David Mamet became a name to be reckoned with.

Meanwhile, Mamet continued to write plays and to accrue recognition in his native city. He was also establishing relationships that would endure through his rising career, one of the most notable being with director Gregory Mosher, who was to stage many of Mamet's works. Under his guidance, *American Buffalo*, set in a Chicago junk store, premièred at the Goodman Theatre's Stage Two in 1975, moving the next year to New York's St Clement's Theatre – winning an Obie Award

– and finally, in 1977, to Broadway, garnering the New York Drama Critics' Circle Award. With this impressive debut, Mamet had now established himself as a playwright of note whose career demanded attention.

In the 1980s, though Mamet continued writing plays, he began to move into the Hollywood arena, where he has since established himself as a noted screenwriter as well as director, producing works ranging from mainstream movies to smaller budget films that more clearly reflect his theatrical concerns and style. His initiation into the Hollywood scene came through director Bob Rafelson, who hired Mamet to write the script for *The Postman Always Rings Twice*. This project was soon followed by scripts for *The Verdict* (directed by Sidney Lumet) and *The Untouchables* (directed by Brian De Palma). Mamet has said that film work has taught him the importance of sticking to plot, as opposed to his usual character- and dialogue-driven plays.

Following his commercial film successes, as well as honing the craft of screenwriting, Mamet wrote and directed two original works: *House of Games* (1987) and *Things Change* (1988), the latter co-authored with Shel Silverstein. In these films, Mamet returns to his dramatic themes of thwarted American dreams, manipulation and con artistry, and the failure of human relationships. *House of Games*, which is based on a story by Mamet and his friend Jonathan Katz, features a woman as the main character, Dr Margaret Ford – the first woman in Mamet's work to enter traditional male realms. A psychiatrist, she is the author of a new best-seller whose title – *Driven: Compulsion and Obsession in Everyday Life* – is semi-autobiographical, since she herself is a tough-minded, ambitious workaholic. Though the men in the film refer to her as a 'whore' and a 'bitch', Ford is confident and assertive, and unlike women in most Mamet plays, she ultimately has the final power in the fatal conclusion.

Things Change, by contrast, is a much gentler, even comic film at times, though it incorporates the world of the Mafia, hit men, betrayal, and double-dealing. Gino, an innocent shoeshine man, has agreed to take the blame for a mob murder he didn't commit in exchange for enough money to return to his native

Sicily and buy a fishing boat – a dream he is to realise *after* serving a jail sentence. But in the end, the inept gangster guarding him (Jerry) is won over by Gino's integrity and outsmarts the Mob.

Mamet's film work has grown so prominent that it has nearly overshadowed his identity as a playwright, with many people recognising him primarily as a scriptwriter and director. Indeed, most of his Hollywood work has been commercially oriented, with credits including *Hoffa*, *Rising Sun*, *The Edge*, *The Spanish Prisoner*, *We're No Angels*, *Wag the Dog*, and *Ronin*. In 1999, in a rather incongruous turn of interest, Mamet directed a film of *The Winslow Boy*, based on the distinguished 1946 Edwardian play by Terence Rattigan; Mamet notes in his introduction to the screenplay that Rattigan's play 'is a work of melodramatic genius'. Mamet has also continued to write and direct films that reflect his theatrical themes and interests and characters, including *State and Main* (2000), about a narcissistic Hollywood director who invades a small New England town to shoot a B-grade film, and *Heist* (2001), whose characters are familiar Mamet figures – deceptive, manipulative and crude.

During the 1980s and 1990s, several of Mamet's own plays were made into television films or motion pictures, with Mamet often writing the screenplays and/or directing, to varying degrees of commercial success. The 1992 film version of *Glengarry Glen Ross* features a powerful cast including Al Pacino, Jack Lemmon, Ed Harris, Alan Arkin and Kevin Spacey. The film also introduces a new character, played by Alec Baldwin, who is clearly an associate of Mitch and Murray from 'downtown', though he is never identified by name, intensifying his sense of ominence. He delivers an intimidating motivational speech, written specifically by Mamet for the film, about the sales contest, and his threatening quality is heightened by a dark night of pouring rain seen through the grimy windows. Not surprisingly, the film also moves outside the play's settings, but only briefly. These scenes include shots of the Chicago elevated rail thundering by, dreary wet streets, and Roma arriving at the office the morning after the break-in, with the presence of police cars portending the disaster inside.

(To commemorate the film's tenth anniversary, a DVD version was released, which includes a short documentary about real-life salesmen – aptly titled *A.B.C.*, the salesmen's motto, 'Always Be Closing' – as well as interviews with some of the actors, a commentary by the film's director James Foley, and a tribute to Jack Lemmon, who had died the previous year. Alan Arkin commented that in the film, 'every single syllable, every stutter, every stammer was scripted'.)

Other Mamet plays that have been made into films include *Homicide* – which confronts the issue of Jewish identity, a theme Mamet's later plays delve into – *The Water Engine*, *A Life in the Theatre* (with Jack Lemmon and Matthew Broderick), *Oleanna* (featuring Mamet's long-time associate William H. Macy), and *American Buffalo* (with Dennis Franz and Dustin Hoffman).

During the 1980s and 1990s, Mamet also turned to writing adaptations of Anton Chekhov's plays and stories, including *The Cherry Orchard*, *Vint*, and *The Three Sisters,* working primarily from literal translations. His adaptation of Chekhov's *Uncle Vanya* was subsequently made into a successful movie, *Vanya on 42nd Street*, under the guidance of the late French legendary director Louis Malle.

Mamet's output of non-fiction was also prolific during this period, with books, essay collections, and reminiscences that include *Writing in Restaurants*, *Some Freaks*, *On Directing Film*, *The Cabin*, *A Whore's Profession*, *Make-Believe Town*, *True and False: Heresy and Common Sense for the Actor*, *On Acting*, children's books, and poetry.

While Mamet continued to write plays reflecting his familiar gritty underworld and male milieu (including *Glengarry Glen Ross* and *Speed-the-Plow*), by the 1990s, his drama was beginning to undergo subtle shifts, giving women more prominent roles as well as straying into the territory of memory, family, and his own Jewish roots. *The Cryptogram*, for instance, is a delicate but unsettling play about a young boy anxiously waiting to go on a camping trip with his father, but who cannot sleep, being haunted by voices and visions, and ultimately learning that his parents are divorcing. (The fact that the play takes place in the 1950s, around the same time that

Mamet's parents divorced, has garnered critical speculation of autobiographical elements in the play.) While the young boy is the central character, the mother is also prominent, serving as a counterpoint to the absence of the father, who is spoken of but never appears, thus accentuating his disappearance from their lives. *The Old Neighborhood*, comprising three short plays – *The Disappearance of the Jews, Jolly* and *Deeny* – is a gentle nostalgic piece that features a middle-aged Bobby Gould (from *Speed-the-Plow*) reminiscing with a friend about his home town in ways that poignantly reveal the disappointments of his present life. The play also includes interactions with Gould's sister and an old girlfriend. Acknowledged as highly autobiographical, *The Old Neighborhood* was described by one critic as his 'most personal, haunted and haunting play'.

Mamet's powerful 1992 play *Oleanna* took audiences by storm, leaving even the playwright bewildered by the reaction and controversy it evoked. Certainly the fact that it dealt with heated current issues of political correctness, sexual harassment, and feminist concerns fuelled this contention, but those themes also reveal how very much Mamet is in touch with the political, social, and cultural climate of contemporary America. Unlike his earlier plays, *Oleanna* places the central characters – John, a professor, and Carol, his student – on an even playing field, with the man and the woman – as Mamet himself has pointed out – both being 'absolutely right' as well as 'absolutely wrong'. While the character of Carol is inevitably implicated through her manipulation of language as a means to attain power (and seems even more virulent in the film version), John is also guilty of a certain superiority, indiscretion, and insensitivity. The fact that no clear-cut resolution is possible provoked audiences into hot debates, and while the woman in the play ultimately wields the power – even though John to some degree has brought about his own downfall – that power has been suspiciously gained and reprehensibly ill-used. Carol's association with some anonymous feminist group has generated some critical response that the play only perpetuates Mamet's image as a misogynist and misrepresents the concepts and ideals of the feminist movement.

At the start of the millennium, Mamet continues to be an

extraordinarily prolific and diverse writer, with his oeuvre now extending into novels and music even as he continues to turn out plays, films, essays, and other works. He has also worked with his friend, the extraordinary magician Ricky Jay, directing him in highly acclaimed productions that featured Jay displaying his astounding and masterful card tricks. (Jay has appeared in a number of Mamet's films.) Mamet also participated in the *Beckett on Film* project, directing a production of *Catastrophe* that aired on public broadcasting stations in 2002.

Mamet's influences are as broad and eclectic as his own work; he is extremely well read in a remarkable range of fields, from economics to philosophy to literature. He has attributed his love of language and reading partly to his father, a lawyer who was deeply interested in semantics and insisted that his children speak clearly and with correct grammar. While Mamet might eschew the term 'intellectual', there is no doubt that his depth and breadth of knowledge is as impressive as the scope of his own body of work.

Mamet's themes

One of Mamet's central themes concerns the flaws and shortcomings of the American dream, its spiritual demise, its economic futility and its unfairness. In his view, it is a myth based not on hard work but on getting something out of nothing, of accruing success through manipulation and deception, thus making economic life in America 'a lottery'. In an interview with James Cook he said, 'The idea that has enslaved all of us is the idea of getting to the top of the heap. Because what that means is exploitation' ('Life of a Salesman', *Forbes*, 21 May 1984). In *The Water Engine* (1978), for example, Mamet challenges the idea that private enterprise can yield personal success. When the protagonist of the play, who invents an engine that will run on water, refuses to sell the plans to a greedy corporation, he and his sister are murdered, affirming the power of big business to quash the dreams and efforts of the individual. In *American Buffalo*, when Don realises that he has sold a buffalo-head nickel – the ultimate symbol of the Western frontier and all that it embodies – for far less than its actual value, he concocts a plan to rob the buyer of what he assumes to be a valuable coin collection, thus getting back not only the valued nickel but a wealth of other items as well. The play that essentially launched Mamet's dramatic career, *American Buffalo* exposes the tawdry side of the American dream through betrayal, misplaced values, sordid business ethics, and the failure of communication – another motif in Mamet's work.

Glengarry Glen Ross (1983), a watershed in Mamet's career and a play he has dubbed a 'gang comedy', again confronts the duplicity of business as well as personal relationships, with language perverted into a tool of manipulation rather than one of clarification and honesty. Even though the salesmen in this play do work hard to succeed, they are still competing with one another, reiterating Mamet's view that one attains the American dream only through another's loss. Hard work is not enough, as the myth purports; the gains are not equally distributed. As in a poker game, the winner takes all and the losers, despite their efforts, are thrown in the trash heap. This backstabbing, look-out-for-number-one mentality is further illustrated in Mamet's 1988 play, *Speed-the-Plow,* about the nature of Hollywood business dealings.

Mamet's preoccupation with the theme of the American dream has provoked comparisons with such playwrights as Arthur Miller and Sam Shepard, who translate their visions of America into very different kinds of drama. Miller's plays, which tend to take place in more mainstream America, rather than its underworld, are infused with a social and moral consciousness, and stress the consequences of one's actions, though like Mamet's work, they also deal with betrayal, selfishness, and profit. In *All My Sons,* for instance, set on the outskirts of an American town, the character of Joe Keller knowingly sells defective aeroplane parts to the Army in order to save his business but allows his partner to be the fall guy and to serve time in prison. Keller claims to be putting family above social obligations, but Keller's son cannot live with this lie and kills himself, as does Keller himself at the end of the play.

Sam Shepard, like Mamet, has been regarded as a distinctly

American playwright whose plays blast the myths perpetrated by magazines, television, and other mass media. However, he tends to use or refer to distinctly American locales more than Mamet – Hollywood, the desert, Los Angeles, the 'sunshine' states of California and Florida, and the Midwest – as well as to incorporate specific details of the American landscape and culture, such as billboards, particular films, television, and crop fields. Shepard's intent seems to be not so much to debunk the American dream directly as to refute it through showing worlds that contradict it, yet his use of myth, surrealism and symbolism also help universalise his plays. In his Pulitzer Prize-winning *Buried Child*, for example, the setting is the 'heartland' of America, the Midwest, with all its connotations of integrity, stalwartness, and family values. But Shepard exposes it all as a façade. The 'Norman Rockwell' setting is soon revealed to be the home of an alcoholic husband, a faith-preaching but harlot wife, children who have been long absent, relatives who don't recognise each other, incestuous relationships, and a murdered baby. Still, for all its bleakness, *Buried Child,* like many of Shepard's plays, exudes a dark humour, and its symbolic use of Greek elements such as the corn god, incest, and infanticide serve to remind us that the 'dysfunctional' family is not solely an American phenomenon.

Another of Shepard's most well-known plays, *True West*, also skews the American dream, also through a seemingly placid setting that turns into a bizarre nightmare. Austin has climbed the proverbial ladder as dictated by American norms: attending college, working hard, getting married and having children, buying a house and a car, dressing nicely, and doing business in a straightforward way. He is writing a screenplay about what he considers the real West, working by candlelight as America's forefathers had done. His brother Lee, who lives on the desert as a vagabond and thief, intrudes on this calm and ordered existence, appropriating Austin's screenplay to write one of his own which, despite his knowledge of the 'true' West, is yet another fictional action film. In the course of the play, Shepard confronts the myth of the American West, as well as the American dream of Hollywood success, though he also explores the dark psyches of the two brothers.

The difficulty of male-female relationships, another pervasive theme in Mamet's work, is closely allied to the issue of power. The theme arises in *Speed-the-Plow*, for example, as Karen carefully coerces an ethical sensibility from Bobby Gould, who fails to realise that she is using her sexual prowess for her own ambitions. *The Woods* investigates this sexual interaction in a more disturbing, yet poignant manner, casting the relationship into a primal Garden of Eden scenario. *Sexual Perversity in Chicago*, on the other hand, attacks the myth of the male ego and male sexuality in a more linguistically brutal way, exposing its destructiveness through what critic Jack Kroll, in *Newsweek,* describes as a 'sleazy sonata of seduction', while *Oleanna,* coming as it did in the wake of the Anita Hill/Clarence Thomas hearings over sexual harassment, clearly touched a national nerve, generating reactions and debates so heated and widespread that even its author was stymied by the uproar.

Violence often pervades Mamet's work, not least because of the way he delves into the underbelly of American society, exploring the seamy side of life as well as the individual's frustrated need for recognition in an uncaring, anonymous society. In *Prairie du Chien*, for instance, a storyteller recounts a rather surreal tale about a jealous farmer who beats and eventually murders his young wife and her lover, a black hired hand, then sets the barn on fire – in which the bodies are found – before hanging himself on the porch of his house. In the brutal *Edmond*, the title character abruptly leaves his wife to try and find a place for himself in this anonymous world but ends up gradually venting his rage on various victims – viciously stabbing an assailant, dallying with whores, unleashing an intense verbal assault upon a woman in the subway who refuses to acknowledge his presence, and eventually murdering a call girl with whom he cannot engage in a spiritual relationship. Mamet has called *Edmond* 'a morality play about modern society'. In *Oleanna*, the frustrating manipulation of language and John's misinterpreted physical gestures cause Carol to charge him with rape and John eventually to physically assault her, while *House of Games*, built around the familiar Mamet themes of game-playing and con artistry, results in the sole woman character murdering the man who has conned her.

Other themes shape Mamet's work as well, including family and personal relationships, breakdown of language, and even – though less often – connection through communication. The gentle play *Duck Variations* (1978), for instance, comprises a series of vignettes between two old men sitting on a park bench, the episodes being loosely connected by their observations on the behaviour and habits of ducks. *A Life in the Theatre* (1978), which one critic describes as 'a love letter to the theatre', is a touching if painful confrontation between a young actor and an ageing one, between old and new methods of acting, and between the differing generational approaches to the craft. *Dark Pony* (1979) is a lovely tale about a father and daughter returning home from a camping trip, the father telling – or more accurately, re-telling – his child a tale about life in the woods. *Reunion*, a kind of companion piece to *Dark Pony*, while not quite so tender, still evokes a poignancy in its depiction of a father and his grown daughter attempting to reconnect after years apart. In plays such as *The Sanctity of Marriage* (1982) and *The Woods* (1987), Mamet pushes further into the realm of communication and relationships, and their often painful failure, a realm that becomes more brutal when Mamet delves into the business ethos of American society.

Mamet and work

The world of work shapes many of Mamet's plays, including *American Buffalo*, *Speed-the-Plow*, *A Life in the Theatre*, and *Oleanna*, as well as *Glengarry Glen Ross*. The venues of the workplaces vary widely: *American Buffalo* takes place in a junk shop, known more respectably as 'Don's Resale Shop'; *Speed-the-Plow*, set primarily in the office of a Hollywood producer, delves into the seamy, self-serving business of movie-making; *A Life in the Theatre* concerns the profession of its title, depicting an older actor and a younger one in scenes alternating between onstage performance and backstage discussions; *Oleanna*, centred on a college campus, explores the concerns, conflicts, and dangers of a professor's career; and *Glengarry Glen Ross* is clearly focused on the work and workplace of the real estate salesmen.

Glengarry Glen Ross has often been compared to Miller's best-known play, *Death of a Salesman*, given the obvious similarities of topics: the distinctively American trade of salesman – considered to be quite respectable, if not admirable and quintessentially American, in the 1950s – weighed against the more current view, vis à vis Mamet, in the 1980s. Furthermore, Miller and Mamet have distinctly negative views of both the profession and the values it purports. But Miller's play focuses more on the moral aspects of the system, the poignancy of the individual who has failed to meet his own expectations, and the thwarting and bending of personal morality to which belief in the system has led. Miller more overtly attacks the American dream through the characters' speeches and emphasis on the effect of work, with Willy expressing his weariness, Linda acting as the ever-supportive and encouraging wife, and his sons Biff and Happy struggling with the false ideals with which their father has infused them. Furthermore, Willy's abandonment by the new young boss because he is old and outdated is not so much because he can't do the job as that a new system of values has supplanted the old one of loyalty.

While *Death of a Salesman* focuses more on the individual and Willy's emotional and mental unravelling – leading to his ultimate suicide – *Glengarry Glen Ross* is very much *about* business: it takes place *in* the office and *on* the job, and even the scenes in the Chinese restaurant involve the transpiring of business. There is no sentimentality in Mamet's play; the characters are brutal, competitive, insensitive, or pathetic. Where *Death of a Salesman* shows us the sorrowful remnants of a man whom society has failed, *Glengarry Glen Ross* shows us characters at work – scheming, manipulating, pleading, and conning. The workplace jargon that dominates the play reflects this obsession, with dialogue never reflecting any personal life outside the office – apart from the brief mention of Levene's daughter. (In the film version, some touches of humanity are included, as when Levene calls the hospital to enquire about his daughter's illness, though even this enquiry highlights the desperation of his need for more money.) The opening of the play focuses on Levene's plea to Williamson for decent leads, while the play's final lines return to that same theme:

> **Aaronow**   Did the leads come in yet?
> **Roma**   No.
> **Aaronow** (*settling into a desk chair*)   Oh, god I hate this job.
> **Roma** (*simultaneous with 'job', going out of the office*)   I'll be at the restaurant.

Even personal concerns, for example when Lingk wants to pull out of the land deal, are addressed through the salesman's verbal barrage, as when Roma smoothly assures him not to worry: '*Forget* the deal . . . you know me. The deal's *dead*. Am I talking about the *deal*? That's *over*. Please. Let's talk about *you*. Come on' (p.55).

Certainly the undercurrent of the play exposes the sordid means of attaining the American dream and suggests the effects that the business ethos has wrought upon the characters, as well as its merciless nature and tragic results, but the play's central focus remains the business itself.

Mamet's language and style

Among the features for which Mamet's plays have been praised, along with their careful and conscious craftsmanship, are his acute ear for the rhythms of everyday speech as well as his skill with subtext, packing meaning into what is left unsaid. Along with his ability to enhance the relationship between language and behaviour are his storytelling ability and the dexterity of his characters at role-playing. These characteristics are evident from his earliest plays, such as *Sexual Perversity in Chicago*, in which the incisive and crude language defines the characters, through much later plays like *Oleanna*, in which language serves as a tool to shift the balance of power, to manipulate, and ultimately to entrap and destroy. Yet Mamet's theatre has sometimes been criticised as short on plot and action, his focus being more on situations that are static and passive. This view, however, overlooks his long-held tenet that the power of language is essential to drive a plot forward. As he said in an interview with Melvyn Bragg on *The South Bank Show* (16 October 1994), 'The best way to tell a story on stage is with words ... If you've gotta put effects on the stage, you can't tell the story with words; you're doing something desperately wrong.' And indeed, the power of Mamet's language does impel something that is gripping and often terrifying.

Glengarry Glen Ross offers an excellent illustration of this potency. From the opening scene, the play's dialogue conveys much tension: Levene is desperate for money and fearful of losing his job; Williamson is a cold-hearted and shady boss, willing to conduct illicit transactions; the sales competition is lethal and ruthless; the attempt at communication is futile and based solely on personal gain. Thus, even before meeting any of the other characters, the terrifying situation in which someone will inevitably be doomed is established through language. The staccato rhythm of the language, the ellipses and the continual interruptions further accentuate this tension. Consider part of the opening exchange between Levene and Williamson:

Williamson ... you didn't close ...
Levene ... I, if you'd *listen* to me. Please. I *closed* the cocksucker. His '*ex*', John, his *ex*, I didn't know he was married ... he, the *judge* invalidated the ...
Williamson Shelly ...
Levene ... and what is that, John? What? Bad *luck*. That's all it is. I pray in your *life* you will never find it runs in streaks. [...]
Williamson (*pause*) What about the other two?
Levene What two?
Williamson Four. You had four leads. One kicked out, one the *judge*, you say ...
Levene ... you want to see the court records? John? Eh? You want to go down ...
Williamson ... no ...
Levene ... do you want to go down-*town* ...?
Williamson ... no ...
Levene ... then ...
Williamson ... I only ...
Levene ... then what is this 'you *say*' shit, what is that? (*Pause.*) What is that ... ?
Williamson All that I'm saying ... (pp.1–2)

The use of italics, the incomplete sentences, the interruptions and other linguistic techniques further highlight Levene's inarticulacy, frustration and desperation.

This linguistic power continues to drive the play, from Roma's suave development of an illusionary intimacy with Lingk (a relationship that could only be established through language), to Moss's equally calculated if less smooth entrapment of Aaronow into his robbery scheme, to Levene's pitiful recounting of his supposed success with the Nyborgs. For Mamet, language *is* drama; language *creates* the drama.

A good example of this slippery but deadly wordplay is the conversation between Moss and Aaronow about robbing the office (Act One, Scene Two), in which Moss deftly manipulates the meanings of 'saying', 'talking' and 'speaking', words which ordinarily are similar. But in Mamet's hands, they become frighteningly different:

> **Aaronow**   Yes. I mean are you actually *talking* about this, or are we just . . .
> **Moss**   No, we're just . . .
> **Aaronow**   We're just '*talking*' about it.
> **Moss**   We're just *speaking* about it. [. . .]
> **Aaronow**   We're not actually *talking* about it. (pp.17–18)

Another method of linguistic deception, illustrated in this same conversation, is answering questions with questions; in this excerpt, the fatal word is 'actually':

> **Aaronow**   So all this, um, you didn't, actually, you didn't actually go talk to Graff.
> **Moss**   Not actually, no.
> *Pause.*
> **Aaronow**   You didn't?
> **Moss**   No. Not actually.
> **Aaronow**   Did you?
> **Moss**   What did I say?
> **Aaronow**   What did you say?

A few lines further on, a similarly baffling exchange takes place:

> **Aaronow**   You're going to steal the leads?
> **Moss**   Have I said that?

Pause.
Aaronow   Are you?
Pause.
Moss   Did I say that?
Aaronow   Did you talk to Graff?
Moss   Is that what I said?

This kind of double talk and lack of communication which
contributes to the view that Mamet's plays are situational
rather than action-oriented, ostensibly places him in the
category of Absurdist theatre. As mentioned above, Mamet's
work has often been compared to that of Harold Pinter –
whose influence Mamet clearly acknowledges and to whom he
dedicated *Glengarry Glen Ross* – as well as Samuel Beckett,
whom Mamet, in an interview, referred to as 'kind of a
demigod to me'. Like the Absurdist playwrights, Mamet makes
use of terse and fragmented dialogue, brutality of language and
action, the failure or circularity of communication, and the
manipulation of language for subversive purposes. Words are
frustrating rather than effective, and the inability to complete a
sentence reflects the frustration of a character's situation.
Lingk's attempt to cancel his contract offers one example of
this, with a specific focus on the potency – or impotency – of
language:

Lingk   I can't negotiate.
Roma   What does that mean?
Lingk   That . . .
Roma   . . . what, what, *say* it to me . . . Say it to me . . .
Lingk   I . . .
Roma   What . . . ?
Lingk   I . . .
Roma   What . . . ? Say the words.
Lingk   I don't have the *power*. (*Pause.*) I said it.
Roma   What power?
Lingk   The power to negotiate. (p.54)

The use of italics, another common feature of Mamet's
dialogue, enhances this anxiety and inarticulacy, with emphasis
on the words 'say' and 'power'; Roma is urging Lingk to
speak, but Lingk feels inept at using language to express what

he is trying to say, suggesting also that he is too honest and naive to use language as a business stratagem.

Similar linguistic patterns and techniques can be seen in other Mamet plays. *American Buffalo*, for instance, incorporates staccato rhythms, italics, circular arguments and the hesitancy of brackets to illustrate the tension between two characters planning a robbery:

> **Don** What if he didn't write it down?
> **Teach** He wrote it down.
> **Don** I know he did. But just, I'm saying, from *another* instance. Some made-up guy from my imagination.
> **Teach** You're saying in the instance of some guy . . .
> **Don** (Some *other* guy . . .)
> **Teach** . . . he didn't write it down?
> *Pause.*
> **Don** Yes.
> **Teach** Well, this is another thing.
> *Pause.*
> You see what I'm saying?
> **Don** Yeah.
> **Teach** It's another matter. The guy, he's got the shit in the safe, he didn't write it *down* . . .
> *Pause.*
> **Don** . . .?
> **Don** Yes?
> **Teach** How do you know he didn't write it down?
> (Methuen, 2002, pp. 77–8)

In *Speed-the-Plow*, Mamet's contribution to the pathology of the movie industry, language utilises similar techniques in Hollywood jargon. This broken exchange between the two movie moguls reflects their shallow, self-centred natures but also, in a world dedicated to profit, their shared assumptions and understanding which allow the merest hints to stand for communication:

> **Fox** Ah. Now that's the *great* part, I'm telling you, when I saw this script . . .
> **Gould** . . . I don't know how it got past us . . .
> **Fox** When they get out of *prison*, the Head Convict's Sister . . .

> **Gould** ... a buddy film, a prison film, Douggie Brown, blah, blah, some girl ...
> **Fox** Action, a social ...
> **Gould** Action, blood, a social theme ...
> **Fox** (*simultaneously with 'theme'*) That's what I'm *saying*, an offbeat ...
> **Gould** Good. Good. Good. Alright. Now: Now: when we go in ...
> **Fox** That's what I'm saying, Bob.
> **Gould** Don't even say it.
> **Fox** Bob:
> **Gould** I understand. (Methuen, 1988, p.13)

Mamet's unique, stylised language drives the tension and action of his plays, defines and mimics personal relationships, and distinguishes his work to the extent that his name, like Pinter's and Beckett's, has been incorporated into the American lexicon as an adjective: Mametian. Like Hemingway, the seeming simplicity of his language is deceptive, for its carefully sculpted style not only creates a distinctive cadence and mesmerising rhythm, it also reflects the broken and disjointed nature of contemporary relationships, the failure of communication in a world increasingly dominated by the lust for money and power, and the loss of community that once bound people together through family and neighbourhoods but that has been fragmented by the intrusion of modern business and technology, the corruption of traditional values, the dominance of bureaucrats and clock-watchers, and the dismantling, neglect or betrayal of American individualism, mythology and dreams.

Characters

Shelly Levene
Perhaps the most pathetic character in the play, Levene is a salesman in his fifties, well past his prime though unwilling to admit it, and desperately in debt due to his daughter's hospital bills. Having once experienced a more personal relationship with his bosses – much like Willy Loman in Miller's *Death of a Salesman* – Levene resents having to beg his younger boss

Williamson for a break. Despite his innate humanitarianism, Levene – once known as 'Levene the Machine' and now hardened by years of thankless and competitive work – deludes himself about his own success and ultimately seals his fate at the end through his foolhardy robbery of the firm.

John Williamson

The cold and calculating manager of the real estate office, Williamson, in his forties, is younger than most of his salesmen. He is a man concerned solely with business and profits, exhibiting no interest in or empathy with any of his employees, an indifference and hardness that appears in his opening refusal to provide Levene with prime leads – though he does consider bribery – and culminates in his final betrayal of Levene as the perpetrator of the robbery.

Dave Moss

A seasoned and particularly insensitive salesman in his fifties, Moss attempts to manipulate the gullible Aaronow into robbing the firm of its leads in a scheme that will profit Moss while assuring himself an alibi. In the end, it is the desperate Levene who commits the crime, implicating Moss as an accomplice. While it's clear that Levene will be charged, Moss's fate is, in the end, left unresolved.

George Aaronow

Also a salesman in his fifties, Aaronow is the sole voice of conscience in the play, not least because of his own naiveté. An inarticulate, fair-minded, but self-deprecating man, Aaronow best expresses the futility of the salesmen's world at the end of the play when he says, 'Oh, god I hate this job.'

Richard Roma

Clearly the smoothest, slickest salesmen of the group, the forty-something Roma is given the prime leads by the office manager

and illustrates his expertise in his interaction with the
vulnerable James Lingk. Roma is an astute example of the role-
player who seamlessly melds caring and mendacity, a quality
that accounts for his success, yet also makes it difficult to
discern if and when he really cares at all about the people with
whom he interacts – as, for example, his seeming empathy with
both Levene, as he encourages him to recount his 'closing' with
the Nyborgs, and Aaronow ('You're a good man, George').

James Lingk

A lonely and naive man in his forties, apparently married to a
practical if domineering wife, Lingk serves as the representative
'victim' in the salesmen's deadly game of selling. He is lured by
the slick-talking Roma into buying a tract of land, but when
his wife learns of the deal, she insists that he back out of it.
Lingk therefore shows up in the real estate office on the
morning of the robbery, and when he learns that his cheque
has been cashed, he desperately leaves to consult his attorney.
Even Lingk's name suggests the valuable 'link' between
salesman and client that drives the business.

Baylen

Though a less prominent character than the others in the play,
Baylen, a detective in his forties, serves as a pivotal figure in
Act Two as he marshals the individual salesmen into the inner
office for interrogation about the robbery. His presence not
only emphasises what has happened during the night but also
measures the reaction of the various salesmen, ranging from
confusion and bewilderment to self-assurance, anger, and
paranoia.

Glengarry Glen Ross in performance

Interestingly, *Glengarry Glen Ross* premièred not in America
but in Britain, opening in the Cottesloe at London's National
Theatre on 21 September 1983, directed by Bill Bryden and
starring Derek Newark (Levene), Karl Johnson (Williamson),

Trevor Ray (Moss), James Grant (Aaronow), Jack Shepherd (Roma), Tony Haygarth (Lingk), and John Tams (Baylen). It won both the Olivier Award and the Society of West End Theatres Award for Best New Play. Response to the play was overwhelmingly positive, and its American dialect posed virtually no problem for theatregoers or critics. Rather, Mamet's infamous use of dialect and fragmented gutter-talk was the subject of praise from many reviewers. Michael Billington (*Guardian*) noted how Mamet 'conjures up a world in which violent words are used to mask fear, shield panic, [and] hide feelings', while John Barber (*Daily Telegraph*) found that the interest lay in 'seeing how the gullible are beguiled, cheated, and cajoled by professional touts who take a manic pride in their ability to sell people pups'. Robert Cushman (*Observer*), concluding that 'Nobody alive writes better American', invoked the 'intoxicating mixture of evasions, pleadings, browbeatings, stonewalling and spiel: the fantastic ear for emphasis and repetition and the interrupting of people who weren't actually saying anything'. Ros Asquith (*City Limits*) defined it as 'a seedy morality play', while Michael Coveney (*Financial Times*) took a political view of the play, commenting, 'What is particularly resonant about the play is its metaphorical exploitation of the post-Nixon break-in paranoia.'

The American première took place the following year at Chicago's Goodman Theatre on 6 February 1984, directed by Mamet's longtime collaborator Gregory Mosher. Two of the salesmen were played by Mike Nussbaum and Joe Mantegna, actors who have long been affiliated with Mamet's work. The play transferred to Broadway's John Golden Theatre on 25 March and was again applauded, with Richard Corliss (*Time*) calling it a 'monstrously entertaining' work that exposes Mamet's 'peddlers caught in the entrepreneurial act', and Jack Kroll (*Newsweek*) describing it as 'a funny and frightening descent into the Plutonic world of sleazy hucksters' in language he describes as 'semantic skullduggery', 'Neanderthal rhapsodies', and a 'parody of philosophic wisdom', making Mamet 'the Aristophanes of the inarticulate'. During rehearsals, Mamet enlisted a number of salesmen to illustrate how the profession worked, noting that whatever product was being marketed, the rules were the same: Attract attention, engage interest and desire, and aim for action. Ascertain the buyer's need (or create one) and fill it, a process that also requires the salesmen to sell themselves. These salesmen also lived by the ABC principle: 'Always Be Closing'.

Again, as with the British critics, the primary praise for the play focused on Mamet's brilliant ear for incisive dialogue. 'I don't know when I've heard on a stage words so eager to be spoken, so charged in rhythm, so juicy to play, so completely "overheard" yet poetic,' wrote David Denby in *Atlantic Monthly*, a sentiment echoed by Clive Barnes (*New York Post*), who said Mamet 'makes poetry out of common usage', raising ordinary speech 'to its basic potential'. Robert Brustein (*The New Republic*) gave the play perhaps one of the most glowing tributes: 'Like *American Buffalo*, *Glengarry Glen Ross* is to my mind a genuine Mamet masterpiece, a play so precise in its realism that it transcends itself and takes on reverberant ethical meanings. It is biting, pungent, harrowing, and funny, showing life stripped of all idealistic pretenses and liberal pieties – a jungle populated with beasts of prey who nevertheless possess the single redeeming quality of friendship.' He went on to praise the sets, describing them as 'brilliantly rendered disaster areas', as well as the costumes, which 'provide an authentic polyester look for men with a weakness for terrible clothes'.

During the ensuing decade, a number of notable productions were launched worldwide, in locations including Tel Aviv, Johannesburg, Dublin, Paris, Italy, Australia, Minneapolis, Tokyo, and Helsinki, as well as in theatres such as Washington DC's Arena Stage and Rhode Island's Trinity Repertory. Gregory Mosher, Mamet's longtime collaborator, directed revivals in San Francisco, Los Angeles, Boston and Chicago. In February 1986, Bill Bryden opened a revival of the play at London's Mermaid Theatre, and in June 1994, a production by director Sam Mendes opened at the Donmar Warehouse, earning stellar reviews. In 2001, Steppenwolf Theatre staged a revival at Chicago's Goodman Theatre, a production which they took to Dublin's Olympia Theatre the following year. There is every indication that Mamet's powerful play will continue to see numerous international stagings in the years to come.

Further Reading

Books by Mamet

Plays

David Mamet Plays: One, Methuen, London, 1994; contains
*Duck Variations, Sexual Perversity in Chicago, Squirrels,
American Buffalo, The Water Engine, Mr Happiness*

David Mamet Plays: Two, Methuen, London, 1996; contains
*Reunion, Dark Pony, A Life in the Theatre, The Woods,
Lakeboat, Edmond*

David Mamet Plays: Three, Methuen, London, 1996; contains
*Glengarry Glen Ross, Prairie du Chien, The Shawl, Speed-
the-Plow*

David Mamet Plays: Four, Methuen, London, 2002; contains
Oleanna, The Cryptogram, The Old Neighborhood

Short Plays and Monologues, Dramatists Play Service, New
York, 1981; contains *All Men Are Whores, The Blue Hour,
In Old Vermont, Litko, Prairie du Chien, A Sermon,
Shoeshine*

Three Plays: Reunion, Dark Pony, The Sanctity of Marriage,
Samuel French, London, 1982

Dramatic Sketches and Monologues, Samuel French, London,
1985

Three Children's Plays, Grove, New York, 1986; contains *The
Poet and the Rent, The Frog Prince, The Revenge of the
Space Pandas*

Three Jewish Plays, Samuel French, London, 1987; contains
*The Disappearance of the Jews, Goldberg Street, The
Luftmensch*

Five Television Plays, Grove, New York, 1990; contains *A
Waitress in Yellowstone, Bradford, The Museum of Science
and Industry Story, A Wasted Weekend, We Will Take You
There*

Boston Marriage, Methuen, London, 2001

Faustus, Methuen, London, 2005
Romance, Methuen, London, 2005

Screenplays
House of Games, David Mamet and Jonathan Katz, Methuen,
London, 1988
'The Spanish Prisoner' and 'The Winslow Boy', Faber, London,
1999
State and Main, Methuen, London, 2001

Selected other works
Writing in Restaurants, Faber, London, 1988
The Cabin: Reminiscence and Diversions, Turtle Bay Books,
New York, 1992
On Directing Film, Faber, London, 1992
A Whore's Profession: Notes and Essays, Faber, London, 1994
Make-Believe Town: Essays and Remembrances, Faber, London,
1996
True and False: Heresy and Common Sense for the Actor,
Faber, London, 1998
*Three Uses of the Knife: On the Nature and Purpose of
Drama*, Methuen, London, 2002

Books and articles on *Glengarry Glen Ross*

Kevin Alexander Boon, 'Dialogue, Discourse and Dialectics: The
Rhetoric of Capitalism in *Glengarry Glen Ross*', *Creative
Screenwriting*, V, 1998, pp.50–7
J. Calhoun, 'Dead End and Musky Jane: Designs for the Film
Version of *Glengarry Glen Ross*', *Theatre Crafts
International*, XXVI, 1992, p.9
Jonathan S. Cullick, 'Always Be Closing: Competition and
Discourse of Closure in David Mamet's *Glengarry Glen
Ross*', *Journal of Dramatic Theory and Criticism*, VIII, 1994,
pp.23–36
Leslie Kane, *David Mamet's 'Glengarry Glen Ross': Text and
Performance*, Garland, New York, 1996

Yun-cheol Kim, 'Degradation of the American Success Ethic: *Death of a Salesman*, *That Championship Season*, and *Glengarry Glen Ross*', *Journal of English Language and Literature*, XXXVII, 1991, pp.233–48

Philip C. Kolin, 'Mitch and Murray in David Mamet's *Glengarry Glen Ross*', *Notes on Contemporary Literature*, XVIII, 1988, pp.3–5

Robert I. Lublin, 'Differing Dramatic Dynamics in the Stage and Screen Versions of *Glengarry Glen Ross*', *American Drama*, X, 2001, pp.38–55

Maria Cristina A. Nasser and Lilian Cristina B. Duarte, 'The Myth of Success in David Mamet's *Glengarry Glen Ross*', *Estudos-Anglo Americanos*, XVII-XVIII, pp.114–21

Jeanne Andrée Nelson, 'So Close to Closure: The Selling of Desire in *Glengarry Glen Ross*', *Essays in Theatre*, XIV, 1996, pp.107–16

Matthew C. Roudane, 'Public Issues, Private Tensions: David Mamet's *Glengarry Glen Ross*', *South Carolina Review*, XIX, 1986, pp.35–47

Janice A. Sauer, Bibliography of *Glengarry Glen Ross*, 1983–1995, in *David Mamet's 'Glengarry Glen Ross': Text and Performance*, Garland, New York, 1996

David Worster, 'How to Do Things with Salesmen: David Mamet's Speech-Act Play', *Modern Drama*, XXXVII, pp.375–90

Hersh Zeifman, 'Phallus in Wonderland: Machismo and Business in David Mamet's *American Buffalo* and *Glengarry Glen Ross*' in *Modern Dramatists: A Casebook of Major British, Irish, and American Playwrights*, Routledge, New York, 2001

Books and articles on Mamet

C.W.E. Bigsby, *David Mamet*, Methuen, London, 1985

C.W.E. Bigsby, 'David Mamet', *A Critical Introduction to Twentieth-Century American Drama 3: Beyond Broadway*, Cambridge University Press, Cambridge, 1982, pp.251–90

C.W.E. Bigsby, 'David Mamet: All True Stories', *Modern*

American Drama, Cambridge University Press, Cambridge, 2000, pp.199–236

Gay Brewer, *David Mamet and Film: Illusion/Disillusion in a Wounded Land*, McFarland, Jefferson, North Carolina, 1993

Dennis Carroll, *David Mamet*, Macmillan, Basingstoke, 1987

Anne Dean, *David Mamet: Language as Dramatic Action*, Fairleigh Dickinson University Press, Rutherford, New Jersey, 1990

Richard Eder, 'David Mamet's New Realism', *New York Times,* 12 March 1978, VI, pp.40 ff

Christopher Hudgins and Leslie Kane (eds), *Gender and Genre: Essays on David Mamet*, Palgrave, New York, 2001

Leslie Kane (ed.), *David Mamet: A Casebook*, Garland, New York, 1992

Leslie Kane (ed.), *David Mamet in Conversation*, University of Michigan Press, Ann Arbor, 2001

Leslie Kane, *Weasels and Wisemen: Ethics and Ethnicity in the Work of David Mamet*, St Martin's Press, New York, 1999

Kimball King (ed.), *Modern Dramatists: A Casebook of Major British, Irish, and American Playwrights*, Routledge, New York, 2001

John Lahr, 'David Mamet: The Art of Theater XI', *Paris Review*, XXXIX, 1997, pp.50–76

Benedict Nightingale, 'Is Mamet the Bard of Modern Immorality?', *New York Times*, 1 April 1984, p.H5

Myles Weber, 'David Mamet in Theory and Practice', *New England Review*, XXI, 2000

Ross Wetzsteon, 'Interview with David Mamet', *Village Voice,* 5 July 1976, pp.101–4

Glengarry Glen Ross

Always be closing
– Practical sales maxim

This play is dedicated to Harold Pinter

Author's Note

David Mamet himself worked for a while in a real estate office in 1969. Here are his comments describing that time.

The office was a fly-by-night operation which sold tracts of undeveloped land in Arizona and Florida to gullible Chicagoans. The firms advertised on radio and television and their pitch was to this effect: 'Get in on the ground floor . . . Beautiful home-sites in scenic/historic Arizona/ Florida. For more information call . . . for our beautiful brochure.' Interested viewers would telephone in for the brochure and their names and numbers were given to me. My job was to call them back, assess their income and sales susceptibility, and arrange an appointment with them for one of the office salesmen.

This appointment was called a *lead* – in the same way that a clue in a criminal case is called a *lead* – i.e. it may lead to the suspect, the suspect in this case being a *prospect*. It was then my job to gauge the relative worth of these leads and assign them to the salesforce. The salesmen would then take their assigned leads and go out on the appointments, which were called *sits* . . . i.e. a meeting where one actually *sits down* with the prospects . . .

So that's the background to the play. We are in a real estate office. There is a sales contest near its end. The four salesmen have only several more days to establish their position on the sales graph, the *board*. The top man wins a Cadillac, the second man wins a set of steak knives, the bottom two men get fired. The competition centers around the *leads*, with each man trying desperately to get the best ones.

Glengarry Glen Ross was first presented in the Cottesloe auditorium of the National Theatre, London, on 21 September 1983 with the following cast:

Shelly Levene, *fifties*	Derek Newark
John Williamson, *forties*	Karl Johnson
Dave Moss, *fifties*	Trevor Ray
George Aaronow, *fifties*	James Grant
Richard Roma, *forties*	Jack Shepherd
James Lingk, *forties*	Tony Haygarth
Baylen, *forties*	John Tams

Directed by Bill Bryden
Designed by Hayden Griffin
Lighting by Andy Phillips
Sound by Caz Appleton

The US première of the play took place at the Goodman Theater of the Arts Institute of Chicago in a Chicago Theater Groups Inc. production on 6 February 1984 with the following cast:

Shelly Levene	Robert Prosky
John Williamson	J. T. Walsh
Dave Moss	James Tolkan
George Aaronow	Mike Nussbaum
Richard Roma	Joe Mantegna
James Lingk	William L. Peterson
Baylen	Jack Wallace

Directed by Gregory Mosher

Glengarry Glen Ross opened on Broadway at the John Golden Theater on 25 March 1984, presented by Elliot Martin, the Shubert Organization, Arnold Berhard and the Goodman Theater. The cast was as follows:

Shelly Levene	Robert Prosky
John Williamson	J. T. Walsh
Dave Moss	James Tolkan
George Aaronow	Mike Nussbaum
Richard Roma	Joe Mantegna
James Lingk	Lane Smith
Baylen	Jack Wallace

Directed by Gregory Mosher
Lighting by Kevin Rigdon
Costumes by Nan Cibula
Sets by Michael Merritt

The three scenes of Act One take place in a Chinese restaurant.
Act Two takes place in a real estate office.

Act One

Scene One

A booth at a Chinese restaurant, **Williamson** *and* **Levene** *are seated at the booth.*

Levene John . . . John . . . John. Okay. John. John. Look: (*Pause.*) The Glengarry Highland's leads, you're sending Roma out. Fine. He's a good man. We know that he is. He's fine. All I'm saying, you look at the *board*, he's throwing . . . wait, wait, wait, he's throwing them *away*, he's throwing the leads away. All that I'm saying, that you're wasting leads. I don't want to tell you your *job*. All that I'm saying, things get *set*, I know they do, you get a certain *mindset* . . . A guy gets a reputation. We know how this . . . all I'm saying, put a *closer* on the job. There's more than one man for the . . . Put a . . . put a *proven man out* . . . and you watch, now *wait* a second – and you watch your *dollar* volumes . . . You start closing them for *fifty* 'stead of *twenty-five* . . . you put a *closer* on the . . .

Williamson Shelly, you blew the last . . .

Levene No. John. No. Let's wait, let's back up here, I did . . . will you please! Wait a second. Please. I didn't 'blow' them. No. I didn't 'blow' them. No. One kicked *out*, one I *closed* . . .

Williamson . . . you didn't close . . .

Levene . . . I, if you'd *listen* to me. Please. I *closed* the cocksucker. His '*ex*', John, his *ex*, *I* didn't know he was married . . . he, the *judge* invalidated the . . .

Williamson Shelly . . .

Levene . . . and what is that, John? What? Bad *luck*. That's all it is. I pray in your *life* you will never find it runs in streaks. That's what it does, that's all it's doing. Streaks. I pray it misses you. That's all I want to say.

Williamson (*pause*)   What about the other two?

Levene   What two?

Williamson   Four. You had four leads. One kicked out, one the *judge*, you say . . .

Levene   . . . you want to see the court records? John? Eh? You want to go down . . .

Williamson   . . . no . . .

Levene   . . . do you want to go down-*town* . . . ?

Williamson   . . . no . . .

Levene   . . . then . . .

Williamson   . . . I only . . .

Levene   . . . then what is this 'you *say*' shit, what is that? (*Pause.*) What is that . . . ?

Williamson   All that I'm saying . . .

Levene   What is this 'you *say*'? A deal kicks out . . . I got to *eat*. *Shit*, Williamson . . . *Shit You*, Moss . . . Roma . . . look at the *sheets* . . . look at the *sheets*. Nineteen *eighty*, eighty-*one* . . . eighty-*two* . . . six months of eighty-two . . . who's there? Who's up there?

Williamson   Roma.

Levene   Under him?

Williamson   Moss.

Levene   Bull*shit*. John. Bull*shit*. April, September 1981. It's *me*. It isn't *fucking* Moss. Due respect, he's an *order* taker, John. He *talks*, he talks a good game, look at the *board*, and it's *me*, John, it's me . . .

Williamson   Not lately it isn't.

Levene   Lately kiss my ass lately. That isn't how you build an org . . . talk, talk to Murray. Talk to Mitch. When we were on Peterson, who paid for his fucking *car*? You talk to him. The *Seville* . . . ? He came in, 'You bought that for me Shelly.' Out of *what*? Cold *calling*. *Nothing*. Sixty-*five*, when we were there, with Glen Ross *Farms*? You call 'em down-town. What was that? *Luck*? That was 'luck'? *Bullshit*, John. You're luck – burning my ass, I can't get a fucking *lead* . . . you think that was luck. My stats for those years? Bull*shit* . . . over that period of time . . . ? Bull*shit*. It wasn't luck. It was *skill*. You want to throw that away, John . . . ? You want to throw that away?

Williamson It isn't me . . .

Levene . . . it isn't you . . . ? Who *is* it? Who is this I'm talking to? I need the *leads* . . .

Williamson . . . after the thirtieth . . .

Levene Bull*shit* the thirtieth, I don't get on the board the thirtieth, they're going to can my ass. I need the leads. I need them now. Or I'm gone, and you're going to miss me, John, I swear to you.

Williamson Murray . . .

Levene . . . you *talk* to Murray . . .

Williamson I have. And my job is to marshall those leads . . .

Levene Marshall the leads . . . marshall the leads? What the fuck, what bus did *you* get off of, we're here to fucking *sell*. *Fuck* marshalling the leads. What the fuck talk is that? What the fuck talk is that? Where did you learn that? In school . . . ? (*Pause.*) That's 'talk', my friend, that's 'talk'. Our job is to *sell*. I'm the *man* to sell. I'm getting garbage. (*Pause.*) You're giving it to me, and what I'm saying is it's *fucked*.

Williamson You're saying that I'm fucked.

Levene Yes. (*Pause.*) I am. I'm sorry to antagonize you.

Williamson Let me . . .

Levene . . . and I'm going to get bounced and you're . . .

Williamson   . . . let me . . . are you listening to me . . . ?

Levene   Yes.

Williamson   Let me tell you something, Shelly. I do what I'm hired to do. I'm . . . wait a second. I'm *hired* to watch the leads. I'm given . . . hold on, I'm given a *policy. My* job is to *do that.* What I'm *told.* That's it. You, wait a second, *anybody* falls below a certain mark I'm not *permitted* to give them the premium leads.

Levene   Then how do they come up above that mark? With *dreck* . . . ? That's *nonsense.* Explain this to me. Cause it's a waste, and it's a stupid waste. I want to tell you something . . .

Williamson   You know what those leads cost?

Levene   The premium leads. Yes. I know what they cost. John. Because I, *I* generated the dollar revenue sufficient to *buy* them. Nineteen senny-*nine,* you know what I made? Senny-*Nine?* Ninety-six thousand dollars. John? For *Murray* . . . For *Mitch* . . . look at the sheets . . .

Williamson   Murray said . . .

Levene   *Fuck* him. *Fuck* Murray. John? You know? You tell him I said so. What does *he* fucking know? He's going to have a 'sales' contest . . . you know what our sales contest used to be? *Money.* A *fortune.* Money lying on the ground. Murray? When was the last time *he* went out on a sit? Sales contest? It's *laughable.* It's cold out there now, John. It's tight. Money is *tight.* This ain't sixty-five. It ain't. It just ain't. See? See? Now, I'm a good *man* – but I need a . . .

Williamson   Murray said . . .

Levene   John. John . . .

Williamson   Will you please wait a second. Shelly. Please. Murray told me: The hot leads . . .

Levene   . . . ah, *fuck* this . . .

Williamson   The . . . Shelly . . . ? (*Pause.*) The hot leads are assigned according to the board. During the contest. *Period.* Anyone who beats fifty per . . .

Levene   That's fucked. That's fucked. You don't look at the fucking *percentage.* You look at the *gross* . . .

Williamson   Either way. You're out.

Levene   I'm out.

Williamson   Yes.

Levene   I'll tell you why I'm out. I'm *out*, you're giving me toilet paper. John. I've *seen* those leads. I saw them when I was at Homestead, we pitched those cocksuckers Rio Rancho nineteen sixty-*nine* they wouldn't buy. They couldn't buy a fucking *toaster.* They're *broke*, John. They're cold. They're deadbeats, you can't judge on that. Even so. Even so. Alright. Fine. Fine. Even so. I go in, FOUR FUCKING LEADS they got their money in a *sock.* They're fucking *Polacks*, John. Four leads. I close two. *Two.* Fifty per . . .

Williamson   . . . they kicked out . . .

Levene   They *all* kick out. You run in *streaks*, pal. *Streaks.* I'm . . . I'm . . . don't look at the *board*, look at *me.* Shelly Levene. *Anyone. Ask* them on Western. Ask Getz at Homestead. Go ask Jerry Graff. You know who I am . . . I NEED A SHOT. I got to get on the fucking board. Ask them. *Ask* them. Ask them who ever picked up a check I was flush. Moss, Jerry Graff, Mitch himself . . . Those guys *lived* on the business I brought in. They *lived* on it . . . and so did Murray, John. You were here you'd of benefitted from it too. And now I'm saying this. Do I want charity? Do I want *pity*? I want *sits.* I want leads don't come right out of a *phonebook.* Give me a lead hotter than that, I'll go in and close it. Give me a chance. That's all I want. I'm going to *get* up on that fucking board and all I want is a chance. It's a *streak* and I'm going to turn it around. (*Pause.*) I need your help. (*Pause.*)

Williamson   I can't do it, Shelly.

Pause.

Levene   Why?

Williamson   The leads are assigned randomly . . .

Levene   *Bullshit, Bullshit,* you assign them . . . What are you *telling* me?

Williamson   . . . apart from the top men on the contest board.

Levene   Then put me on the board.

Williamson   You start closing again, you'll *be* on the board.

Levene   I can't close these leads, John. No one can. It's a joke. Look, look: you put me in with Roma – we'll go out together, him and me, we'll doubleteam 'em . . .

Williamson   Dream on.

Levene   Okay. Okay . . . Just . . . *(Pause.)* John, look: just give me a hot lead. Just give me two of the premium leads. As a 'test', alright? As a 'test'. And I promise you . . .

Williamson   I can't do it, Shel . . .

Levene   I'll give you ten per cent.

Pause.

Williamson   Of what?

Levene   Of my end what I close.

Williamson   And what if you don't close?

Levene   I *will* close.

Williamson   What if you *don't?* Then I'm *fucked.* You see . . . ? Then it's *my* job. That's what I'm *telling* you.

Levene   I *will* close. John, John, ten per cent. I can get hot. You *know* that . . .

Williamson   Not lately you can't . . .

Levene   Fuck that. That's defeatist. Fuck that. Fuck it . . .
Get on my side. *Go* with me. Let's *do* something. You want
to run this office, *run* it.

Williamson   Twenty per cent.

Pause.

Levene   Alright.

Williamson   And fifty bucks a lead.

Levene   John . . . (*Pause.*) Listen. I want to talk to you.
Permit me to do this a second. I'm older than you. A man
acquires a reputation. On the street. What he does when
he's *up*, what he does otherwise . . . I said 'ten', you said
'no'. You said 'twenty'. I said 'fine', I'm not going to fuck
with you, how can I beat that, you tell me? . . . Okay. Okay.
We'll . . . Okay. Fine. We'll . . . Alright, twenty per cent,
and fifty bucks a lead. That's fine. For now. That's fine. A
month or two we'll talk. A month from now. Next month.
After the thirtieth. (*Pause.*) We'll talk.

Williamson   What are we going to say?

Levene   No. You're right. That's for later. We'll talk in a
month. What have you got? I want two sits. Tonight.

Williamson   I'm not sure I have two.

Levene   I saw the board. You've got *four* . . .

Williamson (*snaps*)   I've got *Roma*. Then I've got Moss . . .

Levene   *Bullshit.* They ain't been in the office yet. Give
'em some stiff. We have a deal or not? Eh? Two sits. The
Des Plaines. Both of 'em, six and ten, you can do it . . . six
and ten . . . eight and eleven, I don't give a shit, you set 'em
up? Alright? The two sits in Des Plaines.

Williamson   Alright.

Levene   Good. Now we're talking.

Pause.

Williamson   A hundred bucks.

Pause.

Levene   Now? (*Pause.*) *Now?*

Williamson   Now. (*Pause.*) Yes . . . *When?*

Levene   Ah, *shit*, John . . .

Pause.

Williamson   I wish I could.

Levene   You fucking asshole . . . (*Pause.*) I haven't got it. (*Pause.*) I haven't got it, John. (*Pause.*) I'll pay you tomorrow. (*Pause.*) I'm coming in here with the sales, I'll pay you *tomorrow.* (*Pause.*) I haven't *got* it, when I pay, the *gas* . . . I get back to the hotel, I'll bring it in tomorrow.

Williamson   Can't do it.

Levene   I'll give you thirty on them now, I'll bring the rest tomorrow. I've got it at the hotel. (*Pause.*) John? (*Pause.*) We do that, for chrissake?

Williamson   No.

Levene   I'm asking you. As a favor to me? (*Pause.*) John. (*Long pause.*) John: my *daughter* . . .

Williamson   I can't do it, Shelly.

Levene   Well, I want to tell you something, fella, wasn't long I could pick up the phone, call *Murray* and I'd have your job. You know that? Not too *long* ago. For what? For *nothing.* 'Mur, this new kid burns my ass.' 'Shelly, he's out.' You're gone before I'm back from lunch. I bought him a trip to Bermuda once . . .

Williamson   I have to go . . . (*He gets up.*)

Levene Wait. Alright. Fine. (*He starts going in his pockets for money.*) The one. Give me the lead. Give me the one lead. The best one you have.

Williamson I can't split them.

Pause.

Levene Why?

Williamson Because I say so.

Levene (*pause*) Is that it? Is that *it?* You want to do business that way . . . ?

Williamson *gets up, leaves money on the table.*

Levene You want to do business that way . . . ? Alright. Alright. Alright. Alright. What is there on the other list . . . ?

Williamson You want something off the B list?

Levene *Yeah.* Yeah.

Williamson Is that what you're saying?

Levene That's what I'm saying. Yeah. (*Pause.*) I'd like something off the other list. Which, very least, that I'm entitled to. If I'm still *working* here which for the moment I guess that I am . . . (*Pause.*) What? I'm sorry I spoke harshly to you.

Williamson That's alright.

Levene The deal still stands, our other thing.

Williamson *shrugs; starts out of the booth.*

Levene Good. Mmm. I, you know, I left my wallet back at the hotel. Alright. Mmm. (*Pause.*) Mmm . . . Fine.

Scene Two

A booth at the restaurant. **Moss** *and* **Aaronow** *seated. After the meal.*

Moss   Polacks and deadbeats.

Aaronow   . . . Polacks . . .

Moss   Deadbeats *all.*

Aaronow   . . . they hold on to their money . . .

Moss   All of 'em. They, *hey*: it happens to us all.

Aaronow   Where am I going to work?

Moss   You have to cheer up, George, you aren't out yet.

Aaronow   I'm not?

Moss   You missed a fucking sale. Big deal. A deadbeat Polack. Big deal. How you going to sell 'em in the *first* place . . . ? Your mistake, you shoun'a took the lead.

Aaronow   I had to.

Moss   You had to, yeah. Why?

Aaronow   To get on the . . .

Moss   To get on the board. Yeah. How you goan a get on the board sell'n a Polack? And I'll tell you, I'll tell you what *else.* You listening? I'll tell you what else: don't ever try to sell an Indian.

Aaronow   I'd never try to sell an Indian.

Moss   You get those names come up, you ever get 'em, 'Patel'?

Aaronow   *Mmm* . . .

Moss   You ever get 'em?

Aaronow   Well, I think I had one once.

Moss   You did?

Aaronow   I . . . I don't know.

Moss   You had one you'd know it. *Patel.* They keep coming up. I don't know. They like to talk to salesmen.

(*Pause.*) They're *lonely*, something. (*Pause.*) They like to feel *superior*, I don't know. Never bought a fucking thing. You're sitting down 'The Rio Rancho *this*, the blah blah blah,' 'The Mountain View,' 'Oh yes. My brother told me that . . .' They got a grapevine. Fuckin' Indians, George. Not my cup of tea. Speaking of which I want to tell you something: (*Pause.*) I never got a cup of tea with them. You see them in the restaurants. A supercilious race. What is this *look* on their face all the time? I don't know. (*Pause.*) I don't know. Their broads all look like they just got fucked with a dead *cat*, I don't know. (*Pause.*) I don't know. I don't like it. Christ . . .

Aaronow What?

Moss The whole fuckin' thing . . . The pressure's just too great. You're ab . . . you're absolu . . . they're too important. All of them. You go in the door. I . . . 'I got to *close* this fucker, or I don't eat lunch.' 'Or I don't win the *Cadillac* . . .' . . . we fuckin' work too hard. You work too hard. We all, I remember when we were at Platt . . . huh? Glen Ross Farms . . . *didn't* we sell a bunch of that . . . ?

Aaronow They came in and they, you know . . .

Moss Well, they fucked it up.

Aaronow They did.

Moss They killed the goose.

Aaronow They did.

Moss And now . . .

Aaronow We're stuck with *this* . . .

Moss We're stuck with *this* fucking shit . . .

Aaronow . . . *this* shit . . .

Moss It's too . . .

Aaronow It is.

Moss Eh?

Aaronow   It's too . . .

Moss   You get a bad month, all of a . . .

Aaronow   You're on this . . .

Moss   All of, they got you on this 'board' . . .

Aaronow   I, I . . . I . . .

Moss   Some *contest* board . . .

Aaronow   I . . .

Moss   It's not right.

Aaronow   It's not.

Moss   No.

Pause.

Aaronow   And it's not right to the *customers*.

Moss   I know it's not. I'll tell you, you got, you know, you got . . . what did I learn as a kid on Western? Don't sell a guy one car. Sell him *five* cars over fifteen years.

Aaronow   That's right?

Moss   Eh . . . ?

Aaronow   That's right?

Moss   Goddam right, that's right. Guys come on: 'Oh, the blah blah blah, *I* know what I'll do: I'll go in and rob everyone blind and go to Argentina cause nobody even *thought* of this before.'

Aaronow   . . . that's right . . .

Moss   Eh?

Aaronow   No. That's absolutely right.

Moss   And so they kill the goose, I, I, I'll . . . and a fuckin' *man*, worked all his *life* has got to . . .

Aaronow   . . . that's right . . .

Moss   Cower in his *boots*.

Aaronow (*simultaneously with 'boots'*)   Shoes, boots, yes . . .

Moss   For some fuckin' 'Sell ten thousand and you win the steak knives . . .'

Aaronow   For some *sales* pro . . .

Moss   . . . Sales promotion, 'you *lose*, then we fire your' . . . No. It's *medieval* . . . it's wrong. 'Or we're going to fire your ass.' It's wrong.

Aaronow   Yes.

Moss   Yes, it is. And you know who's responsible?

Aaronow   Who?

Moss   You know who it is. It's Mitch. And Murray. Cause it doesn't have to be this way.

Aaronow   No.

Moss   Look at Jerry Graff. He's *clean*, he's doing business for *himself*, he's got his, that *list* of his with the *nurses* . . . see? You see? That's *thinking*. Why take ten per cent? A ten per cent comm . . . why are we giving the rest away? What are we giving ninety per . . . for *nothing*. For some jerk sit in the office tell you 'Get out there and close.' 'Go win the Cadillac.' Graff. He goes out and *buys*. He pays top dollar for the . . . you see?

Aaronow   Yes.

Moss   That's *thinking*. Now, he's got the leads, he goes in business for *himself*. He's . . . that's what I . . . that's *thinking*! 'Who? Who's got a steady *job*, a couple bucks nobody's touched, who?'

Aaronow   Nurses.

Moss   So Graff buys a fucking list of nurses, one grand – if he paid two I'll eat my hat – four, five thousand nurses, and he's going *wild* . . .

Aaronow   . . . he is?

Moss   He's doing *very* well.

Aaronow   I heard that they were running cold.

Moss   The nurses?

Aaronow   Yes.

Moss   You hear a *lot* of things . . . He's doing very well.
He's doing *very* well.

Aaronow   With River Oaks?

Moss   River Oaks, Brook Farms. *All* of that shit.
Somebody told me, you know what he's clearing *himself*?
Fourteen, fifteen grand a *week*.

Aaronow   Himself?

Moss   That's what I'm *saying*. Why? The *leads*. He's got
the good leads . . . what are we, we're sitting in the shit here.
Why? We have to go to *them* to *get* them. Huh. Ninety per
cent our sale, we're *paying* to the *office* for the *leads*.

Aaronow   The leads, the overhead, the telephones, there's
lots of things.

Moss   What do you need? A *telephone*, some broad to say
'Good morning,' nothing . . . nothing . . .

Aaronow   No, it's not that simple, Dave . . .

Moss   *Yes*. It *is*. It *is* simple, and you know what the hard
part is?

Aaronow   What?

Moss   Starting up.

Aaronow   What hard part?

Moss   Of doing the thing. The dif . . . the difference.
Between me and Jerry Graff. Going to business for yourself.
The hard part is . . . you know what it is?

Aaronow   What?

Moss   Just the *act*.

Aaronow   What act?

Moss   To say 'I'm going on my own.' Cause what you do, George, let me tell you what you do: you find yourself in *thrall* to someone else. And we *enslave* ourselves. To *please*. To win some fucking *toaster* . . . to . . . to . . . and the guy who got there first made *up* those . . .

Aaronow   . . . that's right . . .

Moss   He made *up* those rules, and we're working for *him*.

Aaronow   That's the truth . . .

Moss   That's the *god's* truth. And it gets me depressed. I *swear* that it does. At MY AGE. To see a goddam: 'Somebody wins the Cadillac this month. P.S. Two guys get fucked.'

Aaronow   *Huh.*

Moss   You don't *axe* your sales force.

Aaronow   No.

Moss   You . . .

Aaronow   You . . .

Moss   You *build* it!

Aaronow   That's what I . . .

Moss   You fucking *build* it! Men come . . .

Aaronow   Men come *work* for you . . .

Moss   . . . you're absolutely right.

Aaronow   They . . .

Moss   They have . . .

Aaronow   When they . . .

Moss   Look look look look, when they *build* your business, then you can't fucking turn around, *enslave* them, treat them like *children*, fuck them up the ass, leave them to fend for themselves . . . no. (*Pause.*) No. (*Pause.*) You're absolutely right, and I want to tell you something.

Aaronow   What?

Moss   I want to tell you what somebody should do.

Aaronow   What?

Moss   Someone should stand up and strike *back*.

Aaronow   What do you mean?

Moss   *Somebody* . . .

Aaronow   Yes . . . ?

Moss   Should do something to *them*.

Aaronow   What?

Moss   Something. To pay them back.

Pause.

Someone, someone should hurt them. Murray and Mitch.

Aaronow   Someone should hurt them.

Moss   Yes.

Pause.

Aaronow   How?

Moss   How? Do something to hurt them. Where they live.

Aaronow   What?

Pause.

Moss   Someone should rob the office.

Aaronow   Huh.

Moss   That's what I'm *saying*. We were, if we were that kind of guys, to knock it off, and *trash* the joint, it looks like robbery, and *take* the fuckin' leads out of the files . . . go to Jerry Graff.

Long pause.

Aaronow   What could we get for them?

Moss   What could we *get* for them? I don't know. Buck a *throw* . . . buck-a-half a throw . . . I don't know . . . Hey, who knows that they're worth, what do they *pay* for them? All told . . . must be, I'd . . . three bucks a throw . . . *I* don't know.

Aaronow   How many leads have we got?

Moss   The *Glengarry* . . . the premium leads . . . ? I'd say we got five thousand. Five. Five thousand leads.

Aaronow   And you're saying a fella could take and sell these leads to Jerry Graff.

Moss   Yes.

Aaronow   How do you know he'd buy them?

Moss   Graff? Because I worked for him.

Aaronow   You haven't talked to him.

Moss   No. What do you mean? Have I talked to him about *this*?

Pause.

Aaronow   Yes. I mean are you actually *talking* about this, or are we just . . .

Moss   No, we're just . . .

Aaronow   We're just '*talking*' about it.

Moss   We're just *speaking* about it. (*Pause.*) As an *idea*.

Aaronow   As an idea.

Moss Yes.

Aaronow We're not actually *talking* about it.

Moss No.

Aaronow Talking about it as a . . .

Moss *No.*

Aaronow As a *robbery*.

Moss As a 'robbery'?! No.

Aaronow *Well.* Well . . .

Moss *Hey.*

Pause.

Aaronow So all this, um, you didn't, actually, you didn't actually go talk to Graff.

Moss Not actually, no.

Pause.

Aaronow You didn't?

Moss No. Not actually.

Aaronow Did you?

Moss What did I say?

Aaronow What did you say?

Moss Yes. (*Pause.*) I said 'Not actually'. The fuck you care, George? We're just *talking* . . .

Aaronow We are?

Moss Yes.

Pause.

Aaronow Because, because, you know, it's a *crime*.

Moss That's right. It's a crime. It is a crime. It's also very safe.

Aaronow You're actually *talking* about this?

Moss That's right.

Pause.

Aaronow You're going to steal the leads?

Moss Have I said that?

Pause.

Aaronow Are you?

Pause.

Moss Did I say that?

Aaronow Did you talk to Graff?

Moss Is that what I said?

Aaronow What did he say?

Moss What did he say? He'd *buy* them.

Pause.

Aaronow You're going to steal the leads and sell the leads to him?

Pause.

Moss Yes.

Aaronow What will he pay?

Moss A buck a shot.

Aaronow For five thousand?

Moss However they are, that's the deal. A buck a throw. Five thousand dollars. Split it half and half.

Aaronow You're saying 'me'.

Moss Yes. (*Pause.*) Twenty-five hundred apiece. One night's work, and the job with Graff. Working the premium leads.

Pause.

Aaronow   A job with Graff.

Moss   Is that what I said?

Aaronow   He'd give me a job.

Moss   He would take you on. Yes.

Pause.

Aaronow   Is that the truth?

Moss   Yes. It is, George. (*Pause.*) Yes. It's a big decision. (*Pause*) And it's a big reward. (*Pause.*) It's a big reward. For one night's work. (*Pause.*) But it's got to be tonight.

Aaronow   What?

Moss   What? What? The *leads*.

Aaronow   You have to steal the leads tonight?

Moss   That's *right*, the guys are moving them down-town. After the thirtieth. Murray and Mitch. After the contest.

Aaronow   You're, you're saying so you have to go in there tonight and . . .

Moss   *You* . . .

Aaronow   I'm sorry?

Moss   *You.*

Pause.

Aaronow   Me?

Moss   *You* have to go in. (*Pause.*) *You* have to get the leads.

Pause.

Aaronow   I do?

Moss   Yes.

Aaronow   I . . .

Moss It's not something for nothing, George, I took you in on this, you have to go. That's your thing. I've made the deal with Graff. I can't go. I can't go in, I've spoken on this too much. I've got a big mouth. (*Pause.*) 'The fucking leads' et cetera, blah blah blah '. . . the fucking tight ass company . . .'

Aaronow They'll know when you go over to Graff . . .

Moss What will they know? That I stole the leads? I *didn't* steal the leads, I'm going to the *movies* tonight with a friend, and then I'm going to the Como Inn. Why did I go to Graff? I got a better deal. *Period*. Let 'em prove something. They can't prove anything that's not the case.

Pause.

Aaronow *Dave.*

Moss Yes.

Aaronow You want me to break into the office tonight and steal the leads?

Moss Yes.

Pause.

Aaronow No.

Moss Oh, yes, George.

Aaronow What does that mean?

Moss Listen to this. I have an alibi, I'm going to the Como Inn, why? Why? The place gets robbed, they're going to come looking for *me*. Why? Because I probably did it. Are you going to turn me in? (*Pause.*) George? Are you going to turn me in?

Aaronow What if you don't get caught?

Moss They come to you, you going to turn me in?

Aaronow Why would they come to me?

Moss   They're going to come to *everyone*.

Aaronow   Why would I *do* it?

Moss   You wouldn't, George, that's why I'm talking to you. Answer me. They come to you. You going to turn me in?

Aaronow   No.

Moss   Are you sure?

Aaronow   Yes. I'm sure.

Moss   Then listen to this: I have to get those leads tonight. That's something I have to do. If I'm not at the *movies* . . . if I'm not eating over at the Inn . . . If you don't do this, then *I* have to come in here . . .

Aaronow   . . . you don't have to come in.

Moss   . . . and *rob* the place . . .

Aaronow   . . . I thought that we were only talking . . .

Moss   . . . they *take* me, then. They're going to ask me who were my accomplices.

Aaronow   *Me?*

Moss   Absolutely.

Aaronow   That's ridiculous.

Moss   Well, to the law, you're an accessory. Before the fact.

Aaronow   I didn't ask to be.

Moss   Then tough luck, George, because you are.

Aaronow   Why? *Why*, because you only *told* me about it?

Moss   That's right.

Aaronow   Why are you doing this to me, Dave? Why are you talking this way to me? I don't understand. Why are you doing this at *all* . . . ?

Moss That's none of your fucking business . . .

Aaronow Well, well, well, *talk* to me, we sat down to eat *dinner*, and here I'm a *criminal* . . .

Moss You *went* for it.

Aaronow In the abstract . . .

Moss So I'm making it concrete.

Aaronow Why?

Moss Why? Why *you* going to give me five grand?

Aaronow Do you need five grand?

Moss Is that what I just said?

Aaronow You need money? Is that the . . .

Moss Hey, hey, let's just keep it simple, what I need is not the . . . what do *you* need . . . ?

Aaronow What is the five grand? (*Pause.*) What is the, you said that were were going to *split* five . . .

Moss I lied. (*Pause.*) Alright? My end is *my* business. Your end's twenty-five. In or out. You tell me, you're out you take the consequences.

Aaronow I do?

Moss Yes.

Pause.

Aaronow And why is that?

Moss Because you listened.

Scene Three

The restaurant. **Roma** *is seated alone at the booth.* **Lingk** *is at the booth next to him.* **Roma** *is talking to him.*

Roma   . . . all train compartments smell vaguely of shit. It
gets so you don't mind it. That's the worst thing that I can
confess. You know how long it took me to get there? A long
time. When you *die* you're going to regret the things you
don't do. You think you're *queer* . . . ? I'm going to tell you
something: we're *all* queer. You think that you're a *thief*? So
what? You get befuddled by a middle-class morality . . . ?
Get *shut* of it. Shut it out. You cheated on your wife . . . ?
You *did* it, *live* with it. (*Pause.*) You fuck little girls, so *be* it.
There's an absolute morality? May *be*. And *then* what? If you
think there is, then *be* that thing. Bad people go to hell? I
don't *think* so. If you think that, act that way. A hell exists
on earth? Yes. I won't live in it. That's *me*. You ever take
a dump made you feel you'd just slept for twelve
hours . . . ?

Lingk   Did I . . . ?

Roma   Yes.

Lingk   I don't know.

Roma   Or a *piss* . . . ? A great meal fades in reflection.
Everything else gains. You know why? Cause it's only food.
This shit we eat, it keeps us going. But it's only food. The
great fucks that you may have had. What do you remember
about them?

Lingk   What do I . . . ?

Roma   Yes.

Lingk   Mmmm . . . ?

Roma   I don't know. For *me*, I'm saying, what it is, it's
probably not the orgasm. Some broads, forearms on your
neck, something her *eyes* did. There was a *sound* she made
. . . or, me, lying, in the, I'll tell you: me lying in bed: the
next day she brought me *café au lait*. She gives me a
cigarette, my balls feel like concrete. Eh? What I'm saying,
What is our life: (*Pause.*) it's looking forward or it's looking
back. And that's our life. That's *it*. Where is the *moment*?

(*Pause.*) And what is it that we're afraid of? Loss. What else? (*Pause.*) The *bank* closes. We get *sick*, my wife died on a plane, the stock market collapsed . . . the house burnt down . . . what of these happen . . . ? None of 'em. We worry anyway. What does this mean? I'm not *secure*. How can I be secure? (*Pause.*) Through amassing wealth beyond all measure? No. And what's beyond all measure? That's a sickness. That's a trap. There is no measure. Only greed. How can we act? The right way, we would say, to deal with this: 'there is a one-in-a-million chance that so and so will happen . . . *Fuck* it, it won't happen to *me*' . . . No. We know that's not right, I think, we say the correct way to deal with this is 'There is a one in so-and-so chance this will happen . . . God *protect* me. I am powerless, let it not happen to me . . .' But no to *that*. I say. There's something else. What is it? 'If it happens, AS IT MAY for that is not within our powers, I will *deal* with it, just as I do *today* with what draws my concern today.' I say *this* is how we must act. I do those things which seem correct to me *today*. I trust myself. And if security concerns me, I do that which *today* I think will make me secure. And every day I *do* that, when that day *arrives* that I need a reserve, a) odds are that I have it and, b) the *true* reserve that I have is the strength that I have of *acting each day* without fear. (*Pause.*) According to the dictates of my mind. (*Pause.*) Stocks, bonds, objects of art, real estate. Now: what are they? (*Pause.*) An opportunity. To what? To make money? Perhaps. To *lose* money? Perhaps. To 'indulge' and to 'learn' about ourselves? Perhaps. *So fucking what*? What *isn't*? They're an *opportunity*. That's all. They're an *event*. A guy comes up to you, you make a call, you send in a brochure, it doesn't matter, 'There these *properties* I'd like for you to see.' What does it mean? What you *want* it to mean. (*Pause.*) Money? (*Pause.*) If that's what it signifies to you. Security? (*Pause.*) Comfort? 'Some schmuck wants to make a buck on me'; or, 'I feel a vibration *fate* is calling' . . . all it is is THINGS THAT HAPPEN TO YOU. (*Pause.*) That's all it is. How are they different? (*Pause.*) Some poor newly married guy gets run down by a cab. Some *busboy* wins the

lottery . . . (*Pause.*) All it is, it's a carnival. What's special . . .
what *draws* us . . . ? (*Pause.*) We're all different. (*Pause.*) We're
not the same . . . (*Pause.*) We're not the same . . . (*Pause.*)
Hmmm . . . (*Pause. Sighs.*) It's been a long day. (*Pause.*) What
are you drinking?

Lingk   Gimlet.

Roma   Well, let's have a couple more. My name is
Richard Roma, what's yours?

Lingk   Lingk. James Lingk.

Roma   James. I'm glad to meet you. (*They shake hands.*) I'm
glad to meet you, James. (*Pause.*) I want to show you
something. (*Pause.*) It might mean *nothing* to you . . . and it
might not. I don't know. I don't know anymore. (*Pause. He
takes out a small map and spreads it on a table.*) What is that?
Florida. Glengarry Highlands. Florida. 'Florida. *Bullshit.*'
And maybe that's true; and that's what *I* said: but look *here*:
What is this? This is a piece of land. Listen to what I'm
going to tell you now:

Act Two

The real estate office. Ransacked. A broken plate glass window boarded up, glass all over the floor. **Aaronow** *and* **Williamson** *standing around, smoking.*

Pause.

Aaronow   People used to say that there are numbers of such magnitude that multiplying them by two made no difference.

Pause.

Williamson   Who used to say that?

Aaronow   In school.

Pause.

Baylen, *a detective, comes out of the inner office.*

Baylen   Alright . . . ?

Roma *enters from the street.*

Roma   *Williamson . . . Williamson,* they stole the contracts . . . ?

Baylen   Excuse me, sir . . .

Roma   Did they get my contracts?

Williamson   They got . . .

Baylen   Excuse me, fella.

Roma   . . . did they . . .

Baylen   Would you excuse us, please . . . ?

Roma   Don't *fuck* with me, fella. I'm talking about a fuckin' Cadillac car that you owe me . . .

Williamson   They didn't get your contract. I filed it before I left.

Roma   They didn't get my contracts?

Williamson   They: excuse me . . . (*He goes back into the inner room with the detective.*)

Roma   Oh, *fuck. Fuck.* (*He starts kicking the desk.*) FUCK FUCK FUCK! WILLIAMSON!!! WILLIAMSON!!! (*He goes to the door* **Williamson** *went into, tries the door, it's locked.*) OPEN THE FUCKING . . . WILLIAMSON . . .

Baylen (*coming out*)   Who are you?

Williamson *comes out.*

Williamson   They didn't get the contracts.

Roma   Did they . . .

Williamson   They got, listen to me . . .

Roma   Th . . .

Williamson   Listen to me: they got *some* of them.

Roma   Some of them . . .

Baylen   Who told you . . . ?

Roma   Who told me wh . . . ? You've got a fuckin', you've . . . a . . . who is this . . . ? You've got a *board-up* on the window . . . *Moss* told me.

Baylen (*looking back towards the inner office*)   Moss . . . Who told him?

Roma   How the fuck do *I* know? (*To* **Williamson**.) *What . . . talk* to me.

Williamson   They took *some* of the con . . .

Roma   . . . some of the contracts . . . Lingk. James Lingk. I closed . . .

Williamson   You closed him yesterday.

Roma   *Yes.*

Williamson   It went down. I filed it.

Roma   You did?

Williamson   Yes.

Roma   Then I'm over the fucking top and you owe me a Cadillac.

Williamson   I . . .

Roma   And I don't want any fucking shit and I don't give a shit, Lingk puts me over the top, you filed it, that's fine, any other shit kicks out *you* go back. You . . . *you* reclose it, cause I *closed* it and you . . . you owe me the car.

Baylen   Would you excuse us, please.

Aaronow   I, um, and may, maybe they're in, they're in . . . you should, John, if we're ins . . .

Williamson   I'm sure that we're insured, George . . . (*Going back inside.*)

Roma   Fuck insured. You owe me a car.

Baylen (*stepping back into his room*)   Please don't leave. I'm going to talk to you. What's your name?

Roma   Are you talking to me?

Pause.

Baylen   Yes.

Pause.

Roma   My name is Richard Roma.

Baylen *goes back into the inner room.*

Aaronow   I, you know, they should be insured.

Roma   What do *you* care . . . ?

Aaronow   Then, you know, they wouldn't be so ups . . .

Roma   Yeah. That's swell. Yes. You're right. (*Pause.*) How are you?

Aaronow   I'm fine. You mean the *board*? You mean the *board* . . . ?

Roma   I don't . . . yes. Okay, the board.

Aaronow   I'm, I'm, I'm, I'm fucked on the board. *You.* You see how . . . I . . . (*Pause.*) I can't . . . my mind must be in other places. Cause I can't do any . . .

Roma   *What*? You can't do *what*?

Pause.

Aaronow   I can't close 'em.

Roma   Well, they're old. I saw the shit they were giving you.

Aaronow   Yes.

Roma   Huh?

Aaronow   Yes. They are old.

Roma   They're ancient.

Aaronow   Clear . . .

Roma   Clear Meadows. That shit's dead.

Pause.

Aaronow   It *is* dead.

Roma   It's a waste of time.

Aaronow   Yes. (*Long pause.*) I'm no fucking good.

Roma   That's . . .

Aaronow   Everything I . . . *you* know . . .

Roma   That's not . . . Fuck that shit, George. You're a, *hey*, you had a bad month. You're a good man, George.

Aaronow   I am?

Roma   You hit a bad streak. We've all . . . look at this: fifteen units Mountain View, the fucking things get stole.

Aaronow He said he filed . . .

Roma He filed half of them, he filed the *big* one. All the little ones, I have, I have to go back and . . . ah *fuck*, I got to go out like a fucking schmuck hat in my hand and reclose the . . . (*Pause.*) I mean, talk about a fucking streak, that would sap *anyone's* self-confi . . . I got to go out and reclose all my . . . Where's the phones?

Aaronow They stole . . .

Roma They stole the . . .

Aaronow What. What kind of outfit are we running where . . . where anyone . . .

Roma (*to himself*) They stole the phones.

Aaronow Where *criminals* can come in here . . . they take the . . . They stole the phones.

Roma They stole the leads. They're . . . *Christ.* (*Pause.*) What am I going to do this month? Oh *shit* . . . (*He starts for the door.*)

Aaronow You think they're going to catch . . . where are you going?

Roma Down the street.

Williamson *sticks his head out of the door.*

Williamson Where are you going?

Roma To the restaura . . . what do you fucking . . . ?

Williamson . . . aren't you going out today?

Roma With what? (*Pause.*) With what, John, they took the leads . . .

Williamson I have the stuff from last year's . . .

Roma Oh. Oh. Oh your 'Nostalgia' file, that's fine. No. Swell. Cause I don't have to . . .

Williamson . . . you want to go out today . . . ?

Roma   Cause I don't have to *eat* this month. No. Okay. *Give* 'em to me . . . (*To himself.*) Fucking Mitch and Murray going to shit a br . . . what am I going to *do* all . . .

Williamson *starts back into the office. He is accosted by* **Aaronow**.

Aaronow   Were the leads . . .

Roma   . . . what am I going to *do* all month . . . ?

Aaronow   Were the leads insured?

Williamson (*long suffering*)   I don't know, George, why?

Aaronow   Cause, you know, cause they weren't, I know that Mitch and Murray uh . . .

Pause.

Williamson   What?

Aaronow   That they're going to be upset.

Williamson   That's right. (*Going back into his office. To* **Roma**.) You want to go out today . . . ? (*Pause.*)

Aaronow   He said we're all going to have to go talk to the guy.

Roma   What?

Aaronow   He said we . . .

Roma   To the cop?

Aaronow   Yeah.

Roma   Yeah. That's swell. *Another* waste of time.

Aaronow   A waste of time? Why?

Roma   *Why?* Cause they aren't going to find the guy.

Aaronow   The cops?

Roma   Yes. The cops. No.

Aaronow   They aren't?

Roma   No.

Aaronow   Why don't you think so?

Roma   Why? Because they're *stupid*. 'Where were you last night . . . ?'

Aaronow   Where were you?

Roma   Where was *I*?

Aaronow   Yes.

Roma   I was at home, where were *you*?

Aaronow   At home.

Roma   *See* . . . ? Were you the guy who broke in?

Aaronow   Was I?

Roma   Yes.

Aaronow   No.

Roma   Then don't sweat it, George, you know why?

Aaronow   No.

Roma   You have nothing to hide.

Aaronow (*pause*)   When I talk to the police, I get nervous.

Roma   Yeah. You know who doesn't?

Aaronow   No, who?

Roma   Thieves.

Aaronow   Why?

Roma   They're inured to it.

Aaronow   You think so?

Roma   Yes.

Pause.

Aaronow   But what should I *tell* them?

Roma   The truth, George. Always tell the truth. It's the easiest thing to remember.

Williamson *comes out of the office with leads.* **Roma** *takes one, reads it.*

Roma   *Patel?* Ravidam *Patel?* How am I going to make a living on these deadbeat *wogs?* Where did you get this, from the *morgue?*

Williamson   If you don't want it, give it back.

Roma   I don't 'want' it, if you catch my drift.

Williamson   I'm giving you *three* leads. You . . .

Roma   What's the fucking point in *any* case . . . ? What's the *point?* I got to argue with *you,* I got to knock heads with the *cops,* I'm busting my *balls,* sell your *dirt* to fucking *deadbeats* money in the *mattress,* I come back you can't even manage to keep the contracts safe, I have to go back and close them *again* . . . what the fuck am I wasting my time, fuck this shit. I'm going out and reclose last week's stuff . . .

Williamson   Don't do it, they might find him.

Roma   They might find the guy?

Williamson   Yes.

Roma   Your 'source' tells you that?

Williamson   The word from Murray is: leave them alone. If we have to get a new sig he'll go out himself, he'll be the *President,* just come *in,* from out of *town* . . .

Roma   Okay, okay, okay, gimme this shit. Fine. (*He takes the leads.*)

Williamson   I'm giving you three . . .

Roma   Three? I count *two.*

Williamson   Three.

Roma   Patel? Fuck *you*. Fuckin' *Shiva* handed him a
million dollars, told him 'sign the deal', he wouldn't sign.
And Vishnu, too. Into the bargain. Fuck *that*, John. You
know your business, I know mine. Your business is being an
asshole, and I find out whose fucking *cousin* you are, I'm
going to go to him and figure out a way to have your *ass* . . .
fuck you – I'll wait for the new leads.

Levene *enters.*

Levene   Get the *chalk*. Get the *chalk* . . . get the *chalk*! I
closed 'em! I *closed* the cocksucker. Get the chalk and put me
on the *board*. I'm going to Hawaii! Put me on the Cadillac
board, Williamson! Pick up the fuckin' chalk. Eight units.
Mountain View . . .

Roma   You sold eight Mountain View?

Levene   You bet your ass. Who wants to go to lunch?
Who wants to go to lunch? I'm buying. (*He slaps a contract
down on **Williamson***'s desk.*) Eighty-two fucking grand. And
twelve grand in commission. John. (*Pause.*) On fucking
deadbeat magazine subscription leads.

Williamson   Who?

Levene (*pointing to the contract*)   *Read* it. Bruce and Harriett
Nyborg. (*Looking around.*) What happened here?

Aaronow   Fuck. I had them on River Glen.

Levene *looks around.*

Levene   What happened?

Williamson   Somebody broke in.

Roma   Eight units?

Levene   That's right.

Roma   *Shelly* . . . !

Levene   Hey, big fucking deal. Broke a bad streak . . .

Aaronow   Shelly, the Machine, Levene.

Levene   You . . .

Aaronow   That's great.

Levene   Thank you, George.

Baylen *sticks his head out of the room, calls in 'Aaronow'.*
Aaronow *goes into the side room.*

Levene / Get on the phone, call Mitch . . .

Roma   They took the phones . . .

Levene   They . . .

Baylen   *Aaronow* . . .

Roma   They took the typewriters, they took the leads,
they took the *cash*, they took the *contracts* . . .

Levene   Wh . . . wh . . . Wha . . . ?

Aaronow   We had a robbery.

Pause.

Levene   When?

Roma   Last night, this morning . . .

Pause.

Levene   They took the leads?

Roma   Mmm.

Moss *comes out of the interrogation.*

Moss   Fuckin' asshole.

Roma   What, they beat you with a rubber bat?

Moss   Cop couldn't find his dick two hands and a map.
Anyone talks to this guy's an *asshole* . . .

Roma   You going to turn States?

Moss Fuck you, Ricky. I ain't going out today. I'm going home. I'm going home because nothing's *accomplished* here . . . Anyone *talks* to this guy is . . .

Roma Guess what the Machine did?

Moss Fuck the Machine.

Roma Mountain View. Eight units.

Moss Fuckin' cop's got no right talk to me that way. I didn't rob the place . . .

Roma You hear what I said?

Moss Yeah. He closed a deal.

Roma Eight units. Mountain View.

Moss (*to* **Levene**) You did that?

Levene Yeah.

Pause.

Moss Fuck you.

Roma Guess who?

Moss When . . .

Levene Just now.

Roma Guess who?

Moss You just this morning . . .

Roma Harriett and blah blah Nyborg.

Moss You did that?

Levene Eighty-two thousand dollars.

Pause.

Moss Those fuckin' *deadbeats* . . .

Levene My ass. I told 'em. (*To* **Roma**.) Listen to this: I said . . .

Moss Hey, I don't want to hear your fucking war stories . . .

Roma Fuck *you*, Dave . . .

Levene 'You have to believe in your*self* . . . you,' look, 'alright . . . ?'

Moss (*to* **Williamson**) Give me some leads. I'm going out . . . I'm getting out of . . .

Roma '. . . you have to believe in your*self* . . .'

Moss Na, fuck the leads, I'm going home.

Levene 'Bruce, Harriett . . . Fuck *me*, believe in your*self* . . .'

Roma . . . we haven't got a lead . . .

Moss Why not?

Roma They took 'em . . .

Moss Hey, they're fuckin' garbage any case . . . This whole goddam . . .

Levene '. . . You look around, you say "this one has so-and-so, and I have nothing" . . .'

Moss *Shit.*

Levene '*Why*? Why don't I get the opportunities . . . ?'

Moss And did they steal the contracts . . . ?

Roma Fuck *you* care . . . ?

Levene 'I want to tell you something, Harriett . . .'

Moss . . . the fuck is *that* supposed to mean . . . ?

Levene Will you shut up, I'm telling you this . . .

Aaronow *sticks his head out.*

Aaronow Can we get some coffee . . . ?

Moss How ya doing?

Pause.

Aaronow Fine.

Moss Uh huh.

Aaronow If anyone's going, I could use some coffee.

Levene 'You *do* get the . . .' (*To* **Roma**.) Huh? Huh?

Moss *Fuck* is that supposed to mean?

Levene 'You *do* get the opportunity . . . You *get* them. As *I* do, as *anyone* does . . .'

Moss Ricky? . . . That I don't care they stole the contracts? (*Pause.*)

Levene I got 'em in the kitchen. I'm eating her crumb cake.

Moss What does that mean?

Roma It *means*, Dave, you haven't closed a good one in a month, none of my business, you want to push me to answer you. (*Pause.*) And so you haven't got a contract to get stolen or so forth.

Moss You have a mean streak in you, Ricky, you know that . . .

Levene Rick. Let me tell you. Wait, we're in the . . .

Moss Shut the fuck up. (*Pause.*) Ricky. You have a mean streak in you . . . (*To* **Levene**.) And what the fuck are *you* babbling about . . . ? (*To* **Roma**.) Bring that shit up. Of my volume. You were on a bad one and I brought it up to *you* you'd harbor it. (*Pause.*) You'd harbor it a long long while. And you'd be right.

Roma Who said 'Fuck the Machine'?

Moss '*Fuck the Machine*'? '*Fuck the Machine*'? What is this? *Courtesy* class . . . ? You're *fucked*, Rick – are you fucking *nuts*? You're hot, so you think you're the *ruler* of this place . . . ?! You want to . . .

Levene   Dave . . .

Moss   . . . Shut up. Decide who should be dealt with how?
Is that the thing? I come into the fuckin' office today, I get
humiliated by some jagoff cop. I get accused of . . . I get this
shit thrown in my face by you, you genuine shit, because
you're top name on the board . . .

Roma   Is that what I did? Dave? I humiliated you? My
God . . . I'm *sorry* . . .

Moss   Sittin' on top of the *world*, sittin' on top of the *world*,
everything's fuckin *peach*fuzz . . .

Roma   Oh, and I don't get a moment to spare for a bust-
out *humanitarian* down on his luck lately. Fuck *you*, Dave, you
know you got a big *mouth*, and *you* make a close the whole
place stinks with your *farts* for a week. 'How much you just
ingested,' what a big *man* you are, 'Hey, let me buy you a
pack of gum. I'll show you how to *chew* it.' Your *pal* closes,
all that comes out of your mouth is *bile*, how fucked *up* you
are . . .

Moss   *Who's* my pal . . . ? And what are you, Ricky, huh,
what are you, Bishop *Sheean*? Who the fuck are *you*, Mr
Slick . . . ? What are you, friend to the *workingman*? Big deal.
Fuck *you*, you got the memory a fuckin' *fly*. I never liked you.

Roma   What is this, your farewell speech?

Moss   I'm going home.

Roma   Your farewell to the troops?

Moss   I'm not going home. I'm going to Wis*con*sin.

Roma   Have a good trip.

Moss   Fuck you. Fuck the *lot* of you. Fuck you *all*.

Moss *exits. Pause.*

Roma (*to* **Levene**)   You were saying? (*Pause.*) Come on.
Come on, you got them in the kitchen, you got the stats

spread out, you're in your shirtsleeves, you can *smell* it.
Huh? Snap out of it, you're eating her *crumb* cake.

Pause.

Levene   I'm eating her *crumb* cake . . .

Roma   . . . how was it . . . ?

Levene   From the store.

Roma   . . . fuck *her* . . .

Levene   'What we have to do is *admit* to ourself that we
see that opportunity . . . and *take* it. (*Pause.*) And that's it.'
And we *sit* there . . . (*Pause.*) I got the pen out . . .

Roma   Always Be Closing . . .

Levene   That's what I'm *saying*. The *old* ways. The *old*
ways . . . convert the mother fucker . . . *sell* him . . . *sell* him
. . . *make him sign the check.* (*Pause.*) The . . . Bruce, Harriett . . .
the kitchen, blah: They got their money in *government* bonds
. . . I say *fuck* it, we're going to go the whole route. I plat it
out eight units. Eighty-two grand. I tell them. 'This is now.
This is that *thing* that you've been dreaming of, you're going
to find that suitcase on the train, the guy comes in the door,
the bag that's full of money. This is it, *Harriett* . . .'

Roma (*reflectively*)   Harriett . . .

Levene   *Bruce* . . . 'I don't want to fuck *around* with you. I
don't want to go *round* this, and *pussyfoot* around the thing,
you have to look back on this. I do, too. I came here to do
good for you and me. For *both* of us. Why take an interim
position? *The only arrangement I'll accept* is full investment.
Period. The whole eight units. I know that you're saying "be
safe", I know what you're saying. I know if I left you to
yourselfs, you'd say "come back tomorrow" and when I
walked out that door, you'd make a cup of *coffee* . . . you'd sit
down . . . and you'd think "let's be safe . . ." and not to
disappoint me you'd go *one* unit or maybe two, because
you'd become scared because you'd met possi*bili*ty. But this

won't do, and that's not the subject . . .' Listen to this, I
actually said this: 'That's not the subject of our *evening*
together.' Now I handed them the pen. I held it in my hand.
I turned the contract eight units eighty-two grand. 'Now I
want you to sign.' (*Pause.*) I sat there. Five minutes. Then, I
sat there, Ricky, *twenty-two minutes* by the kitchen *clock.*
(*Pause.*) Twenty-two minutes by the kitchen clock. Not a
word, not a *motion*. What am I thinking? 'My arm's getting
tired'? *No.* I *did* it. Like in the *old* days, Ricky. Like I was
taught . . . Like, like, like I *used* to do . . . I did it.

Roma   Like you taught me . . .

Levene   Bullshit, you're . . . No. That's raw . . . well, if I
did, them I'm *glad* I did. I, *well.* I locked on them. All on
them, nothing on me. All my thoughts are on them. I'm
holding the last thought that I spoke: 'Now is the time.'
(*Pause.*) They signed, Ricky. It was *great.* It was fucking great.
It was like they wilted all at once. No *gesture* . . . nothing.
Like together. They, I swear to God, they both kind of
imperceptibly slumped. And he reaches and takes the pen and
signs, he passes it to her, she signs. It was so fucking solemn.
I just let it sit. I nod like this. I nod again. I grasp his hands.
I shake his hands. I grasp *her* hands. I nod at her like this.
'Bruce . . . Harriett . . .' I'm beaming at them. I'm nodding
like this. I point back in the living-room, back to the
sideboard. (*Pause.*) *I didn't fucking know there was a sideboard
there*!! He goes back, he brings us a drink. Little shotglasses.
A pattern in 'em. And we toast. In silence.

Pause.

Levene   . . . Ah fuck.

Roma   That was a great sale, Shelly.

Pause.

Williamson *sticks his head out of the office.*

Levene   Leads! Leads! Williamson! Send me *out*! Send me
out!

Williamson   The leads are coming.

Levene   *Get* 'em to me!

Williamson   I talked to Murray and Mitch an hour ago. They're coming in, you understand they're a bit *upset* over this morning's . . .

Levene   Did you tell 'em my sale?

Williamson   How could I tell 'em your sale? Eh? I don't have a tel . . . I'll tell 'em your sale when they bring in the leads. Alright? Shelly. Alright? We had a little . . . You closed a deal. You made a good sale. Fine.

Levene   It's better than a good sale. It's a . . .

Williamson   Look: I have a lot of things on my mind, they're coming in, alright, they're very upset, I'm trying to make some *sense* . . .

Levene   All that I'm *telling* you: that one thing you can tell them it's a remarkable sale.

Williamson   The only thing remarkable is who you made it to.

Levene   What does *that* fucking mean?

Williamson   That if the sale sticks, it will be a miracle.

Levene   Why should the sale not stick? Hey, fuck *you*. That's what I'm saying. You have no idea of your job. A man's his job and you're *fucked* at yours. You hear what I'm saying to you? Your 'end of month board' . . . You can't run an office. I don't care. You don't know what it *is*, you don't have the *sense*, you don't have the *balls*. You ever been on a sit? *Ever*? Has this cocksucker ever been . . . you ever sit down with a cust . . .

Williamson   I were you, I'd calm down, Shelly.

Levene   *Would* you? *Would* you . . . ? Or you're gonna *what*, fire me?

Williamson   It's not impossible.

Levene   On an eighty-thousand dollar *day*? And it ain't even *noon*.

Roma   You closed 'em today?

Levene   Yes. I did. This *morning*. (*To* **Williamson**.) What I'm *saying* to you: things can *change*. You *see*? This is where you fuck *up*, because this is something you don't *know*. You can't look down the *road*. And see what's *coming*. Might be someone *else*, John. It might be someone *new*, eh? Someone *new*. And you can't look *back*. Cause you don't know *history*. You ask them. When we were at Rio Rancho, who was top man? A month . . . ? Two months . . . ? Eight months in twelve for three years in a row. You know what that means? You know what that means? Is that *luck*? Is that some, some, some purloined leads? That's *skill*. That's *talent*, that's, that's . . .

Roma   . . . *yes* . . .

Levene   . . . and you don't *remember*. Cause you weren't *around*. That's cold *calling*. Walk up to the door. I don't even know their *name*. I'm selling something they don't even *want*. You talk about soft sell . . . before we had a name for it . . . before we called it anything, we did it.

Roma   That's right, Shel.

Levene   And, and, and, I *did* it. And I put a kid through *school*. She . . . and . . . Cold *calling* fella. Door to door. But you don't know. You don't know. You never heard of a *streak*. You ever heard of 'marshalling your sales force' . . . what are you, you're a *secretary*, John. Fuck *you*. That's my message to you. Fuck you and kiss my ass. You don't like it, I'll go talk to Jerry Graff. Period. Fuck you. Put me on the board. And I want three worthwhile leads today and I don't want any bullshit about them and I want 'em close together cause I'm going to hit them all today. That's all I have to say to you.

Roma He's right, Williamson.

Williamson *goes into a side office. Pause.*

Levene It's not right. I'm sorry, and I'll tell you who's to blame is Mitch and Murray.

Roma *sees something outside the window.*

Roma (*sotto*) Oh Christ.

Levene The hell with him. We'll go to lunch, the leads won't be up for . . .

Roma You're a client. I just sold you five waterfront Glengarry Farms. I rub my head, throw me the cue 'Kenilworth'.

Levene . . . What is it?

Roma Kenilw . . .

James Lingk *enters the office.*

Roma (*to* **Levene**) *I* own the property, my *mother* owns the property, I put her *into* it. I'm going to show you on the plats. You look when you get home A–3 through A–14 and 26 through 30. You take your time and if you still feel.

Levene No, Mr Roma. I don't need the time, I've made a lot of *investments* in the last . . .

Lingk I've got to talk to you.

Roma (*looking up*) Jim! What are you doing here? Jim Lingk, D. Ray Morton . . .

Levene Glad to meet you.

Roma I just put Jim into Black Creek . . . are you acquainted with . . .

Levene No . . . Black *Creek.* Yes. In *Florida*?

Roma Yes.

Levene I wanted to *speak* with you about . . .

Roma   Well, we'll do that this weekend.

Levene   My *wife* told me to look into . . .

Roma   *Beautiful.* Beautiful rolling land. I was telling Jim and Jinny, Ray, I want to tell you something. (*To* **Levene**.) You, Ray, you eat in a lot of restaurants. I know you do . . . (*To* **Lingk**.) Mr Morton's with American Express . . . he's (*To* **Levene**.) I can tell Jim what you do . . .

Levene   Sure.

Roma   Ray is Director of all European Sales and Services for American Ex . . . (*To* **Levene**.) But I'm saying you haven't had a *meal* until you've tasted . . . I was at the Lingks' last . . . as a matter of fact, what was that Service Feature you were talking about . . .

Levene   Which . . .

Roma   'Home Cooking' . . . what did you call it, you said it . . . it was a tag phrase that you had . . .

Levene   Uh . . .

Roma   Home . . .

Levene   Home cooking . . .

Roma   The monthly interview . . . ?

Levene   Oh! for the *magazine* . . .

Roma   Yes. Is this something that I can talk ab . . .

Levene   Well, it isn't coming *out* until the February iss . . . *sure.* Sure, go ahead, Rick.

Roma   You're sure?

Levene   (*nods*)   Go ahead.

Roma   Well, Ray was eating at one of his company's men's home in France . . . the man's French, isn't he?

Levene   No, his *wife* is.

Roma   Ah. Ah, his wife is. Ray: what *time* do you have . . . ?

Levene   Twelve fifteen.

Roma   Oh! My God . . . I've got to get you on the *plane*!

Levene   Didn't I say I was taking the two o' . . .

Roma   No. You said the One. That's why you said we couldn't talk till Kenilworth.

Levene   Oh, my God, you're right! I'm on the One . . . (*Getting up.*) Well, let's *scoot* . . .

Lingk   I've got to talk to you . . .

Roma   I've got to get Ray to O'Hare . . . (*To* **Levene**.) Come on, let's hustle . . . (*Over his shoulder.*) John! Call American Express in *Pittsburgh* for Mr Morton, will you, tell them he's on the one o'clock. (*To* **Lingk**.) I'll see you . . . Christ, I'm sorry you came all the way in . . . I'm running Ray over to O'Hare . . . You wait here, I'll . . . no. (*To* **Levene**.) I'm meeting your man at the Bank . . . (*To* **Lingk**.) I wish you'd phoned . . . I'll tell you, wait: (*To* **Lingk**.) Are you and Jinny going to be home tonight? (*He rubs his forehead.*)

Lingk   I . . .

Levene   Rick.

Roma   What?

Levene   *Kenilworth* . . . ?

Roma   I'm sorry . . . ?

Levene   *Kenilworth.*

Roma   Oh, God . . . Oh, God . . . (**Roma** *takes* **Lingk** *aside, sotto.*) Jim, excuse me . . . Ray, I told you, who he is is *the* Senior Vice-President American Express. His family owns thirty-two per . . . Over the past years I've sold him . . . I can't tell you the dollar amount, but *quite* a lot of land. I promised five *weeks* ago that I'd go to the wife's birthday party in Kenilworth tonight. (*He sighs.*) I *have* to go. You understand. They treat me like a member of the family, so I have to go. It's funny, you know, you get a picture of the Corporation Type Company Man, all business . . . this man, *no*. We'll go out to his home sometime. Let's see. (*He checks his datebook.*) Tomorrow. No. Tomorrow, I'm in L.A. . . . *Monday* . . . I'll take you to lunch, where would you like to go?

Lingk   My wife . . .

Roma *rubs his head.*

Levene (*standing in the door*)   Rick . . . ?

Roma   I'm sorry, Jim. I can't talk now. I'll call you tonight . . . I'm sorry. I'm coming, Ray.

He starts for the door.

Lingk   My wife said I have to cancel the deal.

Roma   It's a common reaction, Jim. I'll tell you what it is, and I know that that's why you married her. One of the reasons is *prudence*. It's a sizeable investment. One thinks *twice* . . . it's also something *women* have. It's just a reaction to the size of the investment. *Monday*, if you'd invite me for dinner again . . . (*To* **Levene**.) This woman can *cook* . . .

Levene (*simultaneously*)   I'm sure she can . . .

Roma (*to* **Lingk**)   We're going to talk. I'm going to *tell* you something. Because (*Sotto.*) there's something about your acreage I want you to know. I can't talk about it now. I really shouldn't. And, in fact, by *law*, I . . . (*He shrugs, resigned.*) The man next to you, he bought his lot at forty-*two*, he phoned to say that he'd *already* had an offer . . . (**Roma** *rubs his head.*)

Levene   Rick . . . ?

Roma   I'm coming, Ray . . . what a day! I'll call you this evening, Jim. I'm sorry you had to come in . . . Monday, lunch.

Lingk   My wife . . .

Levene   Rick, we really have to go.

Lingk   My wife . . .

Roma   Monday.

Lingk   She called the Consumer . . . the Attorney, I don't
know. The Attorney Gen . . . they said we have three
days . . .

Roma   *Who* did she call?

Lingk   I don't know, the Attorney Gen . . . the . . . some
Consumer office, umm . . .

Roma   Why did she do *that*, Jim?

Lingk   I don't know. (*Pause.*) They said we have three
days. (*Pause.*) They said we have three days.

Roma   Three days.

Lingk   To . . . you know. (*Pause.*)

Roma   No I don't know. *Tell* me.

Lingk   To change our minds.

Roma   Of *course* you have three days.

Pause.

Lingk   So we can't talk *Monday* . . .

Pause.

Roma   Jim, Jim, you saw my book . . . I *can't, you* saw my
book . . .

Lingk   But we have to *before* Monday. To get our money
ba . . .

Roma   Three *business* days. They mean three *business* days.

Lingk   Wednesday, Thursday, Friday.

Roma   I don't understand.

Lingk   That's what they are. Three business . . . if I wait till Monday, my time limit runs out.

Roma   You don't count Saturday.

Lingk   I'm not.

Roma   No, I'm saying you don't include Saturday . . . in your three days. It's not a *business* day.

Lingk   But I'm not *counting* it. (*Pause.*) Wednesday. Thursday. Friday. So it would have elapsed.

Roma   What would have elapsed?

Lingk   If we wait till Mon . . .

Roma   When did you write the check?

Lingk   Yest . . .

Roma   What was yesterday?

Lingk   Tuesday.

Roma   And when was that check cashed?

Lingk   I don't know.

Roma   What was the *earliest* it could have been cashed?

Pause.

Lingk   I don't know.

Roma   *Today.* (*Pause.*) *Today.* Which, in any case, it was not, as there were a couple of points on the agreement I wanted to go over with you in any case.

Lingk   The check wasn't cashed?

Roma   I just called down-town, and it's on their desk.

Levene   Rick . . .

Roma   One moment, I'll be right with you. (*To* **Lingk**.) In fact, a . . . *one* point, which I spoke to you of which (*He looks around.*) I can't talk to you about here.

Baylen *puts his head out of the doorway.*

Baylen   Levene!!!

Lingk   I, I . . .

Roma   Listen to me, the *statute*, it's for your protection. I have no complaints with that, in fact, I was a member of the board when we *drafted* it, so quite the *opposite*. It *says* that you can change your mind three working days from the time the deal is closed.

Baylen   Levene!

Roma   Which, wait a second, which is not until the check is cashed.

Baylen   Levene!!

Aaronow *comes out of the* **Detective**'s *office.*

Aaronow   I'm *through*, with *this* fucking mishagas. No one should talk to a man that way. How are you *talking* to me that . . . ?

Baylen   Levene!

Williamson *puts his head out of the office.*

Aaronow   . . . how can you *talk* to me that . . . that . . .

Levene (*to* **Roma**)   Rick, I'm going to flag a cab.

Aaronow   *I* didn't rob . . .

Williamson *sees* **Levene**.

Williamson   Shelly: get in the office.

Aaronow   *I* didn't . . . why should *I* . . . 'Where were you last . . .' is anybody listening to me . . . ? Where's Moss . . . ? Where . . . ?

Baylen   Levene! (*To* **Williamson**.) Is this Lev . . .
(**Baylen** *accosting* **Lingk**.)

Levene (*taking* **Baylen** *into the office*)   Ah. Ah. Perhaps I can advise you on that . . . (*To* **Roma** *and* **Lingk**, *as he exits.*) *Excuse* us, will you . . . ?

Aaronow (*simultaneous with* **Levene**'*s speech above*)   . . . Come in here . . . I *work* here, I don't come in here to be *mistreated* . . .

Williamson   Go to *lunch*, will you . . .

Aaronow   I want to *work* today, that's why I came . . .

Williamson   The leads come in, I'll let . . .

Aaronow   . . . that's why I came in. I thought I . . .

Williamson   Just go to lunch.

Aaronow   I don't *want* to go to lunch.

Williamson   Go to lunch, George.

Aaronow   Where does he get off to talk that way to a working man? It's not . . .

Williamson (*buttonholes him*)   Will you take it outside, *we* have people trying to do *business* here . . .

Aaronow   That's what, that's what, that's what *I* was trying to do. (*Pause.*) That's why I came *in* . . . I meet *Gestapo* tac . . .

Williamson (*going back into his office*)   Excuse me . . .

Aaronow   I meet *Gestapo* tactics . . . I meet *Gestapo* tactics . . . that's not right . . . No man has the right to . . . 'call an attorney', that means you're guilt . . . you're under sus . . . 'Co', he says, 'Cooperate' or we'll go down-town. *That's* not . . . as long as I've . . .

Williamson (*bursting out of his office*)   Will you get out of here? Will you get *out* of here? Will you? I'm trying to run an *office* here. Will you go to lunch? Go to lunch. Will you go to lunch? (*He retreats into his office.*)

Roma (*to* **Aaronow**)   Will you excuse . . .

Aaronow   Where did Moss . . . ? I . . .

Roma   Will you excuse us please?

Aaronow   Uh uh, did he go to the restaurant? (*Pause.*) I . . . I . . . (*He exits.*)

Roma   I'm *very* sorry, Jimmy. I apologize to you.

Lingk   It's not me, it's my wife.

Roma (*pause*)   What is?

Lingk   I told you.

Roma   Tell me again.

Lingk   What's going on here?

Roma   Tell me again. Your wife.

Lingk   I told you.

Roma   You tell me again.

Lingk   She wants her money back.

Roma   We're going to speak to her.

Lingk   No. She told me 'right now'.

Roma   We'll speak to her, Jim . . .

Lingk   She won't listen.

Baylen *sticks his head out.*

Baylen   *Roma.*

Lingk   She told me if not, I have to call the State's Attorney.

Roma   No, no. That's just something she 'said'. We don't have to do that.

Lingk   She told me I *have* to.

Roma   No, Jim.

Lingk   I *do*. If I don't get my *money* back . . .

Williamson *points out* **Roma** *to him.*

Baylen   Roma! (*To* **Roma**.) I'm talking to you . . .

Roma   I've . . . look. (*Generally.*). Will someone get this guy off my back.

Baylen   You have a problem?

Roma   Yes, I have a problem. Yes, I *do*, my fr . . . It's not me that ripped the joint off, I'm doing *business.* I'll be with you in a *while.* You got it . . .? (*He looks back,* **Lingk** *is heading for the door.*) Where are you going?

Lingk   I'm . . .

Roma   Where are you going . . . ? This is *me* . . . This is Ricky, Jim. Jim, anything you *want,* you *want* it, you *have* it. You understand? This is *me.* Something *upset* you. Sit down, now sit down. You tell me what it is. (*Pause.*) Am I going to help you fix it? You're goddamned right I am. Sit down. Tell you something . . . ? *Sometimes* we need someone from *outside.* It's . . . no, sit down . . . Now *talk* to me.

Lingk   I can't negotiate.

Roma   What does that mean?

Lingk   That . . .

Roma   . . . what, what, *say* it. Say it to me . . .

Lingk   I . . .

Roma   What . . . ?

Lingk   I . . .

Roma   What . . . ? Say the words.

Lingk   I don't have the *power.* (*Pause.*) I said it.

Roma   What power?

Lingk   The power to negotiate.

Roma   To negotiate what? (*Pause.*) To negotiate what?

Lingk *This.*

Roma What, 'this'?

Pause.

Lingk The deal.

Roma The 'deal', *forget* the deal. *Forget* the deal, you've got something on your mind, Jim, what is it?

Lingk (*rising*) I can't talk to you, *you* met my wife, I . . .

Pause.

Roma What? (*Pause.*) What? (*Pause.*) What, Jim: I tell you what, let's get out of here . . . let's go get a drink.

Lingk She told me not to talk to you.

Roma Let's . . . no one's going to know, let's go around the *corner* and we'll get a drink.

Lingk She told me I had to get back the check or call the State's Att . . .

Roma *Forget* the deal, Jimmy. (*Pause.*) *Forget* the deal . . . you know me. The deal's *dead.* Am I talking about the *deal?* That's *over.* Please. Let's talk about *you.* Come on. (*Pause.* **Roma** *rises and starts walking toward the front door.*) Come on. (*Pause.*) Come on, Jim. (*Pause.*) I want to tell you something. Your life is your own. You have a contract with your wife. You have certain things you do *jointly,* you have a *bond* there . . . and there are *other* things. Those things are yours. You needn't feel *ashamed,* you needn't feel that you're being *untrue* . . . or that she would abandon you if she knew, this is your life. (*Pause.*) *Yes.* Now I want to *talk* to you because you're obviously upset and that *concerns* me. Now let's go. Right now.

Lingk *gets up and they start for the door.*

Baylen (*sticks his head out of the door*)   Roma . . .

Lingk . . . and . . . and . . .

Pause.

Roma   What?

Lingk   And the check is . . .

Roma   What did I *tell* you? (*Pause.*) What did I say about the three days . . . ?

Baylen   Roma, would you, I'd like to get some lunch . . .

Roma   I'm talking with Mr Lingk. If you please, I'll be back in. (*He checks his watch.*) I'll be back in a while . . . I told you, check with Mr Williamson.

Baylen   The people down-town said . . .

Roma   You call them again. Mr Williamson . . . !

Williamson   Yes.

Roma   Mr Lingk and I are going to . . .

Williamson   Yes. Please. Please. (*To* **Lingk**.) The police (*He shrugs.*) can be . . .

Lingk   What are the police doing?

Roma   It's nothing . . .

Lingk   What are the *police* doing here . . . ?

Williamson   We had a slight burglary last night.

Roma   It was nothing . . . I was telling Mr Lingk . . .

Williamson   Mr Lingk. James Lingk. Your contract went out. Nothing to . . .

Roma   John . . .

Williamson   Your contract went out to the bank.

Pause.

Lingk   You cashed the check?

Williamson   We . . .

Roma   . . . Mr Williamson . . .

Williamson   Your check was cashed yesterday afternoon.
And we're completely insured, as you know, in *any* case.
(*Pause.*)

Lingk (*to* **Roma**)   You cashed the check?

Roma   Not to my knowledge, no . . .

Williamson   I'm sure we can . . .

Lingk   Oh, Christ . . . (*He starts out the door.*) Don't follow
me . . . Oh, Christ . . . (*Pause. To* **Roma**.) I know I've let you
down. I'm sorry. For . . . Forgive . . . for . . . I don't know
anymore. (*Pause.*) Forgive me. (**Lingk** *exits.*) (*Pause.*)

Roma (*to* **Williamson**)   You stupid fucking cunt. *You*,
Williamson . . . I'm talking to *you*, shithead . . . You just cost
me *six thousand dollars*. (*Pause.*) Six thousand dollars. And one
Cadillac. That's right. What are you going to do about it?
What are going to do about it, asshole. You fucking *shit*.
Where did you learn your *trade*. You stupid fucking *cunt*. You
idiot. Whoever told you you could work with *men*?

Baylen   Could I . . .

Roma   I'm going to have your *job*, shithead. I'm going
down-town and talk to Mitch and Murray, and I'm going to
Lemkin. I don't care *whose* nephew you are, who you know,
whose dick you're sucking on. You're going *out*, I swear to
you, you're going . . .

Baylen   Hey, fella, let's get this done . . .

Roma   Anyone in this office lives on their *wits* . . . (*To*
Baylen.) I'm going to be with you in a second. (*To*
Williamson.) What you're hired for is to *help* us – does that
seem clear to you? To *help* us. *Not* to fuck us up . . . to help
men who are going *out* there to try to earn a *living*. You *fairy*.
You company man . . . I'll tell you something else. I hope
you knocked the joint off, I can tell our friend here
something might help him to catch you. (*He starts into the*

room.) You want to learn the first rule you'd know if you ever spent a day in life, you never open your mouth till you know what the shot is. (*Pause.*) You fuckin' *child* . . . (**Levene** *has come out during the diatribe with* **Lingk** *and has sat at the back listening. To* **Levene**.) Don't leave. I have to talk to you. (*To* **Williamson**.) You fucking *child* . . . (**Roma** *goes into the inner room.*)

Levene   You *are* a shithead, Williamson . . . (*Pause.*)

Williamson   Mmm.

Levene   You can't think on your feet you should keep your mouth closed. (*Pause.*) You hear me? I'm *talking* to you. Do you hear me . . . ?

Williamson   Yes. (*Pause.*) I hear you.

Levene   You can't learn that in an office. Eh? He's right. You have to learn it on the streets. You don't *buy* that. You have to *live* it.

Williamson   Mmm.

Levene   *Yes*. Mmm. *Yes. Precisely. Precisely.* 'Cause your partner *depends* on it. (*Pause.*) I'm *talking* to you, I'm trying to tell you something.

Williamson   You are?

Levene   Yes, I am.

Williamson   What are you trying to tell me?

Levene   What I was trying to tell you yesterday. Why you don't belong in this business.

Williamson   Why I don't . . .

Levene   You listen to me, someday you might say, 'Hey . . .' No, fuck that, you just listen what I'm going to say: Your partner *depends* on you. Your partner . . . a man who's your 'partner' *depends* on you . . . you have to go *with* him and *for* him . . . or you're shit, you're *shit*, you can't exist alone . . .

Williamson (*brushing past him*)   Excuse me . . .

Levene   . . . excuse you, *nothing*, you be as cold as you want, but you just fucked a good man out of six thousand dollars and his goddam bonus cause you didn't know the *shot*, if you can do that and you aren't man enough that it gets you, then I don't know what, if you can't take *some thing* from that . . . (*Blocking his way.*) you're *scum*, you're fucking white-bread. You be as cold as you want. A *child* would know it, he's right. (*Pause.*) You're going to make something up, be sure it will *help* or keep your mouth closed.

Pause.

Williamson   Mmm.

Levene *lifts up his arm.*

Levene   Now I'm done with you.

Pause.

Williamson   How do you know I made it up?

Levene (*pause*)   What?

Williamson   How do you know I made it up?

Levene   What are you talking about?

Williamson   You said 'You don't make something up unless it's sure to help.' (*Pause.*) How did you know that I made it up?

Levene   What are you talking about?

Williamson   I told the customer that his contract had gone to the bank.

Levene   Well, hadn't it?

Williamson   No. (*Pause.*) It hadn't.

Levene   Don't *fuck* with me, John, don't *fuck* with me . . . what are you saying?

Williamson   Well, I'm saying this, Shel: Usually I take the contracts to the bank. Last night I didn't. How did you know that? One night a year that I left a contract on my desk. Nobody knew that but *you*. Now how did you know that? (*Pause.*) You want to talk to me, you want to talk to someone *else* . . . because this is *my* job on the line, and you're going to *talk* to me: Now how did you know that contract was on my desk?

Levene   You're so full of shit.

Williamson   You robbed the office.

Levene (*laughs*)   Sure!

Williamson   What'd you do with the leads? (*Pause. He points to the* **Detective***'s room.*) You want to go in there? I tell him what we know, he's going to dig up *something* . . . You got an alibi last night? You better have one. What did you do with the leads? If you tell me what you did with the leads, we can talk.

Levene   I don't know what you are saying.

Williamson   If you tell me where the leads are, I won't turn you in. If you *don't*, I am going to tell the cop you stole them, Mitch and Murray will see that you go to jail.

Levene   They wouldn't do that.

Williamson   They would and they will. What did you do with the leads? I'm walking in that door – you have five seconds to tell me: or you are going to jail.

Levene   I . . .

Williamson   I don't care. You understand? *Where are the leads?* (*Pause.*) Alright. (**Williamson** *goes to open the office door.*)

Levene   I sold them to Jerry Graff.

Williamson   How much did you get for them? (*Pause.*) How much did you get for them?

Levene   Five thousand. I kept half.

Williamson   Who kept the other half?

Pause.

Levene   Do I have to tell you? (*Pause.* **Williamson** *starts to open the door.*) Moss.

Williamson   *That* was easy *wasn't* it?

Pause.

Levene   It was his idea.

Williamson   *Was* it?

Levene   I . . . I'm sure he got more than the five, actually.

Williamson   Uh huh?

Levene   He told me my share was twenty-five.

Pause.

Williamson   Mmm.

Levene   Okay: I, look: I'm going to make it worth your while. I am. I turned this thing around. I closed the *old* stuff, I can do it again. *I'm* the one's going to close 'em. *I* am! *I* am! Cause I turned this thing a . . . I can do *that*, I can do *anyth* . . . last night. I'm going to tell you, I was ready to Do the Dutch. Moss gets me, 'Do this, we'll get well . . .' Why not? Big fuckin' deal. I'm hoping to get caught. To put me out of my . . . (*Pause.*) But it *taught* me something. What it taught me, that you've got to get *out* there. Big deal. So I wasn't cut out to be a thief. I *was* born for a salesman. And now I'm back, and I got my *balls* back . . . and, you know, John, you have the *advantage* on me now. Whatever it takes to make it right, we'll make it right. We're going to make it right.

Williamson   I want to tell you something, Shelly. You have a big mouth.

Pause.

Levene   What?

Williamson   You've got a big mouth, and now I'm going to show you an even bigger one. (*He starts towards the* **Detective***'s door.*)

Levene   Where are you going, John? . . . you can't do that, you don't want to do that . . . hold, hold on . . . hold on . . . wait . . . wait . . . wait . . . (*He pulls money out of his pockets.*) Wait . . . uh, look . . . (*He starts splitting the money.*) Look, twelve, twenty, two, twen . . . twenty-five hundred, it's . . . take it. (*Pause.*) Take it . . . (*Pause.*) Take it!

Williamson   No, I don't think so, Shel.

Levene   I . . .

Williamson   No, I think I don't want your money. I think you fucked up my office. And I think you're going away.

Levene   I . . . what? Are you, are you, that's why . . . ? are you nuts? I'm . . . I'm going to *close* for you, I'm going to . . . (*Thrusting money at him.*) Here, here, I'm going to *make* this office . . . I'm going to be back there Number One . . . Hey, hey, hey! This is only the beginning . . . List . . . list . . . listen. Listen. Just one moment. List . . . here's what . . . here's what we're going to do. Twenty per cent. I'm going to give you twenty per cent of my sales . . . (*Pause.*) Twenty per cent. (*Pause.*) For as long as I am with the firm. (*Pause.*) Fifty per cent. (*Pause.*) You're going to be my partner. (*Pause.*) Fifty per cent. Of all my sales.

Williamson   What sales?

Levene   What sales . . . ? I just *closed* eight-two *grand* . . . Are you fuckin' . . . I'm *back* . . . I'm *back*, this is only the beginning.

Williamson   Only the beginning . . .

Levene   Abso . . .

Williamson   Where have you been, Shelly? Bruce and Harriett Nyborg. Do you want to see the *memos* . . . ? They're nuts . . . they used to call in every week. When I was with Webb. And we were selling Arizona . . . they're nuts . . . did you see how they were *living*? How can you delude yours . . .

Levene   I've got the check . . .

Williamson   Frame it. It's worthless.

Pause.

Levene   The check's no good?

Williamson   You stick around I'll pull the memo for you. (*He starts for the door.*) I'm busy now . . .

Levene   . . . their check's no good? They're nuts . . . ?

Williamson   Call up the bank. *I* called them.

Levene   You did?

Williamson   I called them when we had the lead . . . four months ago. (*Pause.*) The people are insane. They just like talking to salesmen. (**Williamson** *starts for the door.*)

Levene   Don't.

Williamson   I'm sorry.

Levene   *Why?*

Williamson   Because I don't like you.

Levene   John: John: . . . my *daughter* . . .

Williamson   Fuck you.

Roma *comes out of the* **Detective**'s *door.* **Williamson** *goes in.*

Roma (*to* **Williamson**)   *Asshole* . . . (*To* **Levene**.) Guy couldn't find his fuckin' couch the *living-room* . . . Ah, Christ . . . what a day, what a day . . . and I haven't even had a cup of *coffee* . . . Jagoff John opens his mouth he blows my Cadillac . . . (*He sighs.*) I swear . . . it's not a world of men . . . it's not a world of men, Machine . . . it's a world of clock watchers, bureaucrats, office holders . . . What it is, it's a fucked-up world . . . there's no adventure *to* it . . . (*Pause.*)

Dying breed. Yes it is. (*Pause.*) We are the members of a dying breed. That's . . . that's . . . I want to talk to you. I've wanted to talk to you for some *time* actually . . . seriously. Did you eat today?

Levene   Me?

Roma   Yes.

Levene   No.

Roma   No? Come on, we're going to swing by the Chinks, we got to talk.

Levene   I think I'd better stay here for a while.

Roma   Okay: Two things, then. One . . . I been thinking about this for a *month*, I said 'the Machine . . . There's a fellow I could *work* with,' never, isn't that funny? I never did a thing. Now: That shit that you were slinging on the guy today was *very* good, and excuse me it isn't even my *place* to *say* that to you that way; I've been on a hot streak, so big deal. What I'm saying, it was *admirable* and, so was the *deal* that you closed. Now listen: there's things I could *learn* from you – you see, I *knew* we'd work well together – Here's what I was thinking: we Team Up. We team up, we go out together, we split everything right down the middle . . .

Baylen *sticks his head out of the room.*

Baylen   Mr *Levene* . . . ?

Roma   . . . fifty-fifty. Or we could go down the street. You know, we could go *anywhere* . . .

Baylen   Would you step in here, please . . . ?

Roma   So let's put it *together*? Okay? (*Pause.*) Shel? Say 'okay'.

Levene (*pause*)   Hmm . . .

Baylen   Mr Levene, I think we have to talk.

Roma   I'm going to the Chinks. You're done, come down, we're going to smoke a cigarette.

Levene   I . . .

Baylen *comes over to him and forcefully leads him into the room.*

Baylen   . . . get in the room.

Roma   Hey, hey, hey, *easy* friend. That's the 'Machine'. That is Shelly The Machine *Lev* . . .

Baylen   Come on. Get in the goddamn *room* . . .

Levene   I . . .

Roma   I'll be at the resta . . .

Baylen *and* **Levene** *have disappeared into the next room and the door is slammed. Pause.*

Roma   Williamson: listen to me: when the *leads* come in . . . listen to me: when the *leads* come in I want my top two off the list. For *me*. My usual two. Anything you give *Levene* . . .

Williamson   . . . I wouldn't worry about it.

Roma   Well I'm *going* to worry about it, and so are you, so you shut up and listen. (*Pause.*) I GET HIS ACTION. My stuff is *mine*, whatever *he* gets, I'm talking half. You put me in with him.

Aaronow *enters.*

Aaronow   Did they . . . ?

Roma   You understand?

Aaronow   Did they catch . . . ?

Roma   Do you understand? My stuff is mine, his stuff is ours.

Williamson   Mmm.

Aaronow   Did they find the guy who broke into the office yet?

Roma   No. *I* don't know . . .

Pause.

Aaronow   Did the leads come in yet?

Roma   No.

Aaronow (*settling into a desk chair*)   Oh, god I hate this job.

Roma (*simultaneous with 'job', going out of the office*)   I'll be at the restaurant.

Notes

1 *leads*: in salesmen's lingo, 'leads' mean the names of
   promising clients, who may be willing and financially able
   to purchase the product – in this case, parcels of land. (See
   Author's Note.) Lists of leads may also be bought from
   another company.
   on the board: again, in salesmen's lingo, the 'board' is a
   bulletin board of some kind where the achievements – i.e.,
   the sales – of the salesmen are posted for everyone to see,
   thus intensifying the competition among the employees in
   the contest to win the Cadillac.
   closer . . . closing: the mantra of salesmen is 'ABC: Always
   Be Closing'. To 'close' a deal means to finalise the sale, to
   ensure the sale by having the client sign the contract or
   agreement. The salesman's commission depends on this and
   the more contracts that he or she is able to 'close', the
   greater his or her income, and the higher his or her status
   rises as a capable and accomplished salesperson.
   One kicked out: this phrase means that one client pulled
   out of the deal and decided not to sign the contract and
   buy the land.
   it runs in streaks: Levene is arguing that when bad luck
   happens, it carries on for a while, with one bit of bad luck
   followed by another. When the 'streak' breaks, then he will
   be making successful sales once again.

2 *do you want to go down-town . . .?*: throughout this play,
   the phrase 'down-town' has an ominous and threatening
   meaning, since that is where the main headquarters of the
   firm are located, and the idea of confronting the big bosses
   of the firm is very intimidating.
   look at the sheets: Levene is referring to the records of past
   sales, arguing that he was one of the top salesmen and that
   now he simply needs a break to regain his status. He is

trying to persuade Williamson to give him some good leads
so that he can get back up on the board.

Murray . . . Mitch: these are the two men who head the
real estate firm and who work in the office down-town.

on Peterson: the estate that the salesmen were selling some
time before.

3   *Seville*: a make of American car by Chevrolet.

Cold calling: a phone call or a visit directly to a potential
customer, soliciting business, without having made prior
contact, in other words, not a 'lead'.

stats: statistics, figures.

I don't get on the board: meaning 'if I don't get on the
board' – an example of how words are missed in the play
in rapid dialogue.

marshall those leads: Williamson is in charge of distributing
the leads to the various salesmen, so he can choose who
will receive the more promising prospects and who will
receive leads that are likely not to yield any results. Levene
is arguing – begging, at this point – to be given some of
the best leads, while Williamson is saying that Levene is no
good any more as a salesman and that the good leads
would be wasted on him; furthermore, he adds that he's
not allowed to give premium leads to salesmen who fall
below a certain level of success.

bounced: fired.

4   *dreck*: a slang word for rubbish, and in this case, worthless
leads.

a sit: this is another term salesman use, referring to a
meeting between the salesman and the prospective client,
where, as Mamet points out in the Author's Note, 'one
actually *sits down* with the prospects'.

5   *I saw them when I was at Homestead . . . Rio Rancho*:
Levene is referring to a time when he worked for another
sales firm, trying to sell lots in an area known as Rio
Rancho. He is arguing that the leads Williamson wants to
give him are names that he had seen before, when he was
working for Homestead, and that those names are no good
– they are 'cold'. Again, he is trying to persuade
Williamson to give him some worthwhile leads so that he

can make a sale.

They're fucking Polacks: throughout the play there are
racial remarks about different ethnic groups who are unable
or unwilling to buy any land. In this case, Levene uses the
derogatory term 'Polack', meaning Poles, to imply that
these people are too stupid and/or too poor to afford any
property.

Getz . . . Jerry Graff: managers of other real estate firms
either where Levene has worked or who are familiar with
Levene's sales ability – or so Levene claims. Jerry Graff will
figure prominently in the play later on, since he is the man
to whom Moss proposes to sell the firm's stolen leads –
assuming the burglary goes through.

who ever picked up a check I was flush: when making sales
and doing well financially, Levene always paid restaurant
bills for colleagues.

7 *Give 'em some stiff*: a worthless lead or a deadbeat.

8 *John: my daughter*: Levene's daughter is in hospital, and
Levene is trying to play on Williamson's sympathy, since
the medical costs are adding to his already heavy burden of
debt.

10 *Polacks and deadbeats*: more abuse for people who are
worthless for making a sale, either because they are stingy
or poor.

don't ever try to sell an Indian: Moss's remark, which is
echoed by Aaronow, is another ethnic slur, referring to
people from India, not to native Americans. Moss goes on
to say that when a name like 'Patel' comes up, which is
clearly an Indian name, such a person should be avoided.
He further adds that they just 'like to talk to salesmen' but
they are never going to buy anything.

11 *You're ab . . . you're absolu . . .*: the broken and incomplete
language which permeates this whole conversation between
Moss and Aaronow indicates both a genuine failure to
articulate and a more conscious manipulation of language
that Moss will use to draw Aaronow into his scheme for
robbing the office. Aaronow is particularly inarticulate,
especially when compared with the smooth, unbroken talk
of Ricky Roma. This style of incomplete and interrupted

sentences is also characteristic of much of Mamet's work, indicating both the failure of language – but sometimes a form of communication in spite of its failure – and its misuse to manipulate and con people rather than to communicate and connect.

They killed the goose: the salesmen continually use clichés, slang, and crude language. This phrase – from 'the goose that laid the golden egg' – refers to the fact that some Indians who had agreed to buy parcels of land in an area known as Glen Ross Farms (undoubtedly worthless swampland) had backed out of the deal. It also suggests that the bosses exerted too much pressure, spoiling the tactics of the salesforce who would have brought in the money.

14   *River Oaks, Brook Farms*: Moss is referring to tracts of land that Jerry Graff is selling. Graff has gone into business for himself rather than working as a salesman for another firm, and Moss tells Aaronow that Graff is making a great deal of money – although whether that is actually true, or whether Moss is just bluffing Aaranow, is not quite clear.

15   *in thrall to someone else*: in servitude, submission, or bondage to someone else, as opposed to being your own boss. In this whole conversation, Moss and Aaronow are expressing anger at the fact that when they make sales, they receive only a ten per cent commission, whereas the firm receives ninety per cent of the deal. Since the salesmen do all the work to earn the money, they feel their cut of the profit should be much higher than ten per cent.

You don't axe your sales force: in the contest that the firm of Mitch and Murray is now sponsoring, the two salesmen who make the lowest number of sales will be fired. Moss is making the point that firing salesmen is bad for morale; the idea is to 'build' a strong sales force rather than get rid of people.

17   *We're just 'talking' about it*: this interchange between Moss and Aaronow illustrates the duplicity of language, which is one of the trademarks of Mamet's work. Moss is carefully crafting the conversation to manipulate Aaronow into

agreeing to be part of the planned robbery, without
Aaronow's realising what he is doing. The interchange is
also an example of how language is used to manipulate
rather than to communicate, and the distinction between
words such as 'talking' and 'speaking' highlights the
nuances of language and how such subtle differences can
convey weighty implications and consequences.
Furthermore, the answering of questions with questions in
this conversation illustrates another technique for avoiding
making direct, complete, and definite statements – another
way for characters to avoid committing themselves to a
particular position or belief. Rather, the characters dance
around the subject and never confront it directly.

23 *Because you listened*: again, the culmination of this
conversation illustrates how Moss has drawn the
unsuspecting Aaronow into his robbery scheme through the
manipulation of language. He implies that Aaronow is now
an accomplice because he listened to Moss outline his plan
and thus is complicit in the planned robbery. Aaronow, of
course, is too naive to realise what has happened to him.

24 Ricky Roma's smooth, controlled, and carefully constructed
conversation is one indication of what separates him from
the other salesmen and what makes him so effective. In
contrast to the pleading, broken language of Levene, or the
disjointed conversation between Aaronow and Moss, Roma
exhibits a command of language, long, unbroken, articulate
monologues, which he uses to lure James Lingk into a
seemingly friendly relationship, ultimately persuading him to
purchase the land he is commissioned to sell. Furthermore,
Roma is talking about 'men' stuff, another way to engage
Lingk in a gender-oriented intimacy. In short, Roma is the
ultimate smooth-talker, a quality that is both despicable
and, as a salesman, quite useful. Through Roma, Mamet
illustrates another way to use the power of language to
manipulate and deceive.

25 *schmuck*: Yiddish slang for a jerk or fool.
busboy: a low-paid worker who clears and resets tables in
restaurants.

Act Two

27 Roma's reaction to the possibility that the contract he had persuaded James Lingk to sign has been stolen provides a good follow-up to his persuasive tactics towards the gullible Lingk. Whereas the previous night's conversation had been intimate and confidential, seemingly sincere, Roma's rage that the contract might have been stolen – and thus his commission gone – highlights the contrast between his apparently sincere concern to do something useful for Lingk and the actual self-interested nature of this exchange. The fact that Williamson lies to Roma about the contract being safe further underscores the duplicity of language that permeates the whole organisation.

30 Roma is a sympathetic character in part because of the genuine interest he shows to some of his fellow salesmen, such as Aaronow, reassuring him that he is not a bad salesman; rather, he has just been given bad leads and he's 'a good man'.

34 *wogs*: another racial slur against those of Indian nationality.

35 *Shiva . . . Vishnu*: Shiva, a Hindu god of destruction and regeneration, and Vishnu, the deity of preservation. Roma continues his disparaging references to Indian people, saying that even if their sacred gods instructed an Indian to buy land he would not follow their instructions. Shiva and Vishnu, along with the creator Brahma, make up the sacred triad of the Hindu religion.
Mountain View: like Glengarry Highlands, another sham but romantic-sounding piece of real estate that the salesmen are hustling.
the Machine: Aaronow's nickname for Shelly implies that he is indomitable.

36 *You going to turn States?*: a phrase referring to 'state's evidence', meaning that a participant or accomplice in a crime gives evidence in return for leniency in sentencing. Whether Roma is just being sarcastic with Moss, or whether he has some sense that Moss is the guilty party, is not clear.

39 The vitriolic exchange between Moss and Roma implies

that Moss's nerves are on edge as a result of the break-in
and reveal his jealousy for Roma's success as a salesman.
His dismissal of the pitiful Levene and Levene's attempt to
trumpet his own sales triumph further illustrate his own
self-absorption and temper. In contrast, Roma's willingness
to listen to Levene narrate how he closed the deal with the
Nyborgs indicates both a shred of humanity as well as the
attentiveness to people that makes him a successful con
man.

40 *what are you, Bishop Sheean?*: Moss is referring to Bishop
Fulton Sheen, an American Catholic clergyman who had a
popular worldwide radio show, *The Catholic Hour*
(1930–52), and gained further prominence with a television
programme, *Life is Worth Living*, that ran 1951–65. It is
revealing that Mamet chooses a religious figure known
largely through the newly developing media, which lend
themselves to distortion and manipulation.

41 *government bonds*: a very safe, long-term form of
investment.
plat: map or chart out the parcels of land and their
features.

44 Levene's newfound confidence, based on his large sale to
the Nyborgs, is expressed in his bold confrontation with
Williamson, his demand for good leads, and his recounting
of the days when his 'cold calling' yielded profitable results.

45 Roma's quick thinking when he sees Lingk approaching the
office has him ask Levene to pretend to be a major
customer who has just made a large land purchase. He says
that Levene is to give him the cue word 'Kenilworth' to
indicate that they have to leave, thus buying time for Roma
to let the contract become official before Lingk can cancel
it. The subsequent 'performance' also indicates the
salesmen's ability to improvise, a major element in their
success. Furthermore, the theatrical conspiracy deepens the
connection between Levene and Roma – particularly for
Levene, a desperate and failing man who admires Roma's
success.
I wanted to speak with you about . . . : the continual
distinctions throughout the play between such words as

'speak', 'talk', 'discuss', and similar terms, indicate the fine nuances that Mamet uses to illustrate how language can be finessed and manipulated to imply different meanings and responses. It also illustrates his brilliance at recognising how a single word can have multiple meanings, depending on the choice of word, the context in which it is used, and the vagueness or clarity in which it is cast.

51 *mishagas*: a Yiddish term for 'craziness'.

61 *Do the Dutch*: steal the leads and split them fifty-fifty with Moss.

64– It is ironic that at this point Roma, the top salesman,
65 should offer to team up with Levene, expressing his admiration of Levene's old sales techniques. However, it transpires that this is not the purely friendly suggestion it appears – Roma is scheming to take a share of the good leads he imagines Levene will be entitled to, while keeping his own from Levene.

Questions for Further Study

1 What does the buying and selling of real estate in *Glengarry Glen Ross* tell us about aspects of the so-called 'American dream'?

2 'Mamet focuses on the loss of spirituality and community in American life as well as the degrading effects of American business and materialism.' Discuss *Glengarry Glen Ross* in the light of this comment.

3 To what extent does the humour of *Glengarry Glen Ross* undermine or complement the play's ostensibly critical content?

4 In what ways is role-playing used in *Glengarry Glen Ross*?

5 Does the overt naturalism of *Glengarry Glen Ross* serve simply to present 'a slice of life' and, therefore, to 'naturalise' the events and situations the play describes as, in some sense, just the way things are or is it the source of the play's particular strengths?

6 'For Mamet, language *is* drama; language *creates* the drama.' Discuss, with reference to *Glengarry Glen Ross*.

7 Comment on Mamet's use of emphasis and ellipsis and the importance of what is left unsaid.

8 'Mamet makes poetry out of common usage' (Clive Barnes, *New York Post*). Do you think this is true of *Glengarry Glen Ross*?

9 'Underneath the staccato language, there is always a muddy river of intentions, desires and old frustrations which connect the disordered fragments on the surface. A sewage system which makes the city work' (Dominic Dromgoole). How appropriate a description of the world of *Glengarry Glen Ross* is this?

10 How, in production, would you seek to ensure that the 'subtext' of the opening page of *Glengarry Glen Ross* was understood by an audience who might otherwise easily fail to appreciate the significance of what is being said? Are

there other areas of the play where special care might be
necessary?

11 'In Mamet's drama there is a complete absence of human
sympathy and an attendant incapacity for an audience to
empathise with either character or situation.' Discuss, with
reference to Glengarry Glen Ross.

12 Assess the significance of off-stage characters and the off-
stage world in Glengarry Glen Ross.

13 What distinctions, if any, does Glengarry Glen Ross seek to
make between 'talking', 'speaking', 'saying' and 'telling' and
how 'telling' are these distinctions?

14 Does there seem to be a feminine element of any
significance in the predominantly male machismo world of
Glengarry Glen Ross?

15 Whose methods would best suit a production of Glengarry
Glen Ross and why – those of Stanislavski, Brecht, a
combination of the two or those of a different theorist
altogether?

16 The salesman's slogan is 'Always be closing'. Does
Glengarry Glen Ross itself suffer from 'closure' in being
less open-ended than it might be?

17 In what ways does Mamet deploy language to suggest
either dominance or submission and are these the only
possibilities held out for human interaction in Glengarry
Glen Ross?

18 What forms of racism does Glengarry Glen Ross touch on
and how does the play treat the issues?

19 According to the nineteenth-century French journalist and
socialist Pierre Joseph Proudhon, 'Property is theft'. Is this
relevant to an understanding of Glengarry Glen Ross as,
specifically, a political play?

20 Glengarry Glen Ross is dedicated to Harold Pinter. In what
ways does the play's use of language compare or contrast
with that of its dedicatee? You might like to look at the
predominantly all-male worlds of The Dumb Waiter or The
Homecoming by way of comparison.

KAREN C. BLANSFIELD is Assistant Professor in the
Department of Dramatic Art at the University of North
Carolina, Chapel Hill, and a resident dramaturg. She is the
author of a book on O. Henry and a forthcoming book on
Michael Frayn. Her articles, essays and reviews have appeared
in several books, including *Gender & Genre: Essays on David
Mamet, Encyclopedia of Modern Drama, Contemporary Gay
American Poets and Playwrights, Companion to American
Drama, Woody Allen: A Casebook* and *Literature and Law*, as
well as many journals, newspapers and magazines. She is Vice-
President of the David Mamet Society.

Methuen Drama Student Editions

Jean Anouilh *Antigone* • John Arden *Serjeant Musgrave's Dance*
Alan Ayckbourn *Confusions* • Aphra Behn *The Rover*
Edward Bond *Lear* • Bertolt Brecht *The Caucasian Chalk Circle*
Life of Galileo • *Mother Courage and her Children*
The Resistible Rise of Arturo Ui • *The Threepenny Opera*
Anton Chekhov *The Cherry Orchard* • *The Seagull* • *Three Sisters*
Uncle Vanya • Caryl Churchill *Serious Money* • *Top Girls*
Shelagh Delaney *A Taste of Honey* • Euripides *Elektra* • *Medea*
Dario Fo *Accidental Death of an Anarchist* • Michael Frayn *Copenhagen*
John Galsworthy *Strife* • Nikolai Gogol *The Government Inspector*
Robert Holman *Across Oka* • Henrik Ibsen *A Doll's House* • *Ghosts*
Hedda Gabler • Charlotte Keatley *My Mother Said I Never Should*
Bernard Kops *Dreams of Anne Frank* • Federico García Lorca
Blood Wedding • *Doña Rosita the Spinster* (bilingual edition) • *The House
of Bernarda Alba* • (bilingual edition) • *Yerma* (bilingual edition) • David
Mamet *Glengarry Glen Ross* • *Oleanna* • Patrick Marber *Closer* • John
Marston *The Malcontent* • Joe Orton *Loot* • Luigi Pirandello *Six
Characters in Search of an Author* • Mark Ravenhill *Shopping and
F***ing* • Willy Russell *Blood Brothers* • *Educating Rita* • Sophocles
Antigone • *Oedipus the King* • Wole Soyinka *Death and the King's
Horseman* • August Strindberg *Miss Julie* • J. M. Synge *The Playboy
of the Western World* • Theatre Workshop *Oh What a Lovely War*
Timberlake Wertenbaker *Our Country's Good* • Arnold Wesker *The
Merchant* • Oscar Wilde *The Importance of Being Earnest* • Tennessee
Williams *A Streetcar Named Desire* • *The Glass Menagerie*

Methuen Drama Modern Plays

include work by

Edward Albee
Jean Anouilh
John Arden
Margaretta D'Arcy
Peter Barnes
Sebastian Barry
Brendan Behan
Dermot Bolger
Edward Bond
Bertolt Brecht
Howard Brenton
Anthony Burgess
Simon Burke
Jim Cartwright
Caryl Churchill
Complicite
Noël Coward
Lucinda Coxon
Sarah Daniels
Nick Darke
Nick Dear
Shelagh Delaney
David Edgar
David Eldridge
Dario Fo
Michael Frayn
John Godber
Paul Godfrey
David Greig
John Guare
Peter Handke
David Harrower
Jonathan Harvey
Iain Heggie
Declan Hughes
Terry Johnson
Sarah Kane
Charlotte Keatley
Barrie Keeffe

Howard Korder
Robert Lepage
Doug Lucie
Martin McDonagh
John McGrath
Terrence McNally
David Mamet
Patrick Marber
Arthur Miller
Mtwa, Ngema & Simon
Tom Murphy
Phyllis Nagy
Peter Nichols
Sean O'Brien
Joseph O'Connor
Joe Orton
Louise Page
Joe Penhall
Luigi Pirandello
Stephen Poliakoff
Franca Rame
Mark Ravenhill
Philip Ridley
Reginald Rose
Willy Russell
Jean-Paul Sartre
Sam Shepard
Wole Soyinka
Simon Stephens
Shelagh Stephenson
Peter Straughan
C. P. Taylor
Theatre Workshop
Sue Townsend
Judy Upton
Timberlake Wertenbaker
Roy Williams
Snoo Wilson
Victoria Wood

Methuen Drama Contemporary Dramatists

include

John Arden (two volumes)
Arden & D'Arcy
Peter Barnes (three volumes)
Sebastian Barry
Dermot Bolger
Edward Bond (eight volumes)
Howard Brenton
 (two volumes)
Richard Cameron
Jim Cartwright
Caryl Churchill (two volumes)
Sarah Daniels (two volumes)
Nick Darke
David Edgar (three volumes)
David Eldridge
Ben Elton
Dario Fo (two volumes)
Michael Frayn (three volumes)
John Godber (three volumes)
Paul Godfrey
David Greig
John Guare
Lee Hall (two volumes)
Peter Handke
Jonathan Harvey
 (two volumes)
Declan Hughes
Terry Johnson (three volumes)
Sarah Kane
Barrie Keefe
Bernard-Marie Koltès
 (two volumes)
Franz Xaver Kroetz
David Lan
Bryony Lavery
Deborah Levy
Doug Lucie

David Mamet (four volumes)
Martin McDonagh
Duncan McLean
Anthony Minghella
 (two volumes)
Tom Murphy (five volumes)
Phyllis Nagy
Anthony Neilson
Philip Osment
Gary Owen
Louise Page
Stewart Parker (two volumes)
Joe Penhall
Stephen Poliakoff
 (three volumes)
David Rabe
Mark Ravenhill
Christina Reid
Philip Ridley
Willy Russell
Eric-Emmanuel Schmitt
Ntozake Shange
Sam Shepard (two volumes)
Wole Soyinka (two volumes)
Simon Stephens
Shelagh Stephenson
David Storey (three volumes)
Sue Townsend
Judy Upton
Michel Vinaver
 (two volumes)
Arnold Wesker (two volumes)
Michael Wilcox
Roy Williams (two volumes)
Snoo Wilson (two volumes)
David Wood (two volumes)
Victoria Wood

Methuen Drama World Classics

include

Jean Anouilh (two volumes)
Brendan Behan
Aphra Behn
Bertolt Brecht (eight volumes)
Büchner
Bulgakov
Calderón
Čapek
Anton Chekhov
Noël Coward (eight volumes)
Feydeau
Eduardo De Filippo
Max Frisch
John Galsworthy
Gogol
Gorky (two volumes)
Harley Granville Barker
   (two volumes)
Victor Hugo
Henrik Ibsen (six volumes)
Jarry

Lorca (three volumes)
Marivaux
Mustapha Matura
David Mercer (two volumes)
Arthur Miller (five volumes)
Molière
Musset
Peter Nichols (two volumes)
Joe Orton
A. W. Pinero
Luigi Pirandello
Terence Rattigan
   (two volumes)
W. Somerset Maugham
   (two volumes)
August Strindberg
   (three volumes)
J. M. Synge
Ramón del Valle-Inclán
Frank Wedekind
Oscar Wilde